Black Flag

50 Warning Signs of Abuse

By

H G Tudor

All Rights Reserved

Copyright 2016

Black Flag: 50 Warning Signs of Abuse

By

H G Tudor

All rights reserved. No part of this book may be reproduced, stored in a retrieval system, or transmitted in any form or by any means, electronic, mechanical, photocopying, recording, or otherwise, without the express written permission of the publisher.

Published by Insight Books

Introduction

When you become ensnared in the grip of a relationship with a narcissist, you will be subjected to abuse. Some of this abuse occurs during seduction but never feels like abuse because it takes the form of wonderful and delightful behaviour which when judged in isolation anybody would regard it as something pleasant. It is actually invariably part of a manipulative front which is opened up against a target in order to con, dupe and defraud them by causing them to fall in love with the narcissist. These methods may come with compliments, loving words, gifts, assistance and support but they are all based on a false premise. These methods are sweet, fragrant and delightful but they mask a more sinister and nefarious aim, that of seducing and ensnaring the narcissist's target. The reality however is that the victim's do not notice this abusive manipulation of them and are carried along on a wave of false love and affection. These abuses appear as red flags and I have detailed more about those in **Red Flag: 50 Warning Signs of Narcissistic Seduction.**

Once this seduction period ends, the victim is subjected to a variety of further abusive manipulative techniques. Some of these are so subtle that the victim does not notice. Others are brutal and very noticeable, although the victim does not realise the full extent and effect of the abusive treatment in terms of eroding their capabilities to cope, controlling them and undermining their attempts to escape this treatment. Not all of these abusive behaviours are the sole preserve of the narcissist and therefore the instances detailed below are just as applicable to those who are engaged with an abusive individual who may or may not be a narcissist. They are however always prevalent with someone who is a narcissist and will always be used in order to achieve the narcissist's aims of extracting negative fuel from the victim, controlling them, diminishing their capability to deal with the abuse and therefore remain in situ and leave them in a position whereby they are nearly destroyed. Many, many victims do not recognise what is happening to them, they may recognise some behaviours but make excuses for it and therefore do not really see what is happening and in many instances they do not know why this behaviour is being exhibited towards them nor the actual effects of it. Accordingly, victims remain in these abusive relationships for far longer than they ought to do, with significant and far-reaching effects on their health and well-being.

This is not a compendium of the abusive techniques that are deployed by narcissists and other abusers, that can be found in **Manipulated** and **The Devil's Toolkit**. Instead, this book is providing you with the indicators that abusive behaviour is taking place or is about to take place. You may have heard of such things as triangulation, projection and gas lighting but what do those concepts actually look like in the context of relationship with an abusive individual. So often people see a type of behaviour, they realise it seems odd and they cannot make sense of it. They do not realise that it is actually a form of abuse and they even less understand why this is done and what the abuser hopes to achieve in behaving in this manner There will be some reference to the types of abusive behaviours that are detailed in the books I have just mentioned, but this is done from the perspective of enabling you to understand how this can be seen. What is the flag that is flying which shows you that this particular form of abuse is being used against you or a person that you are about and love? These flags are always evident. I have labelled them as black flags by reason that firstly a flag is an indicator and black as a consequence of the foul behaviour that is occurring.

People will recognise these black flags in retrospect. They always do. These black flags however are rarely heeded in the context of an abusive relationship and especially not so in the context of a relationship with a narcissist because of the following: -

1. The victim has been indoctrinated to think that their abuser is a wonderful and caring person. Accordingly, they will make excuses for this person's

abuse, such as they are tired, stressed, over worked, ill, not sleeping well, have financial concerns, have a lot on at work and so forth;

2. The victim has been exposed to the powerfully seductive influence of the golden period and believes that the period when they are being abused and devalued is an aberration which will be overcome and that the relationship will return to the status of the golden period once again. This expectation and hope is a form of manipulation that is used against the victim. A victim will live in hope and occasionally be given a glimpse of the golden period again only to find it snatched away again. They will suddenly find that twenty or more years have passed and they are still living in hope of returning to the golden period. This misplaced hope is extremely powerful at masking the reality of the situation that the abused finds themselves in;

3. Often the victim, being an independent and intelligent person does not want to admit that they have made a mistake and therefore they do not want to embarrass themselves or feel ashamed for having been taken in. They will, remarkably choose to endure the ongoing abuse (coupled with a desire to return to the golden period) rather than escape it;

4. External pressures cause the abused to remain in situ. The narcissist is skilled at creating a façade that other people accept and believe in that he or she is pleasant, caring, brilliant, successful and a good person. Accordingly, friends and family may place considerable pressure on the abused individual to remain with the narcissist (often for their own selfish reasons) rather than allow the victim to escape;

5. Most victim of narcissists are empathic individuals who are honest, decent caring and compassionate. They would rather stay to try to help the narcissist overcome his penchant for abusive behaviour than walk away. Indeed, this need to heal and fix is often overwhelming and the individual will want to help the narcissist. They may even feel guilty if they left the

narcissist. This compulsion results in them recognising some of the black flags but remaining nevertheless;

6. The victim may be co-dependent. More can be read about this in **Chained: The Narcissist's Co-Dependent.** In essence, the victim, often unaware of their co-dependency feels that they cannot survive without the narcissist and therefore remain in situ, notwithstanding their recognition of the various black flags;

7. The narcissist is a very persuasive and charming creature. Even if the victim thinks they have identified a black flag, the narcissist will do much to confuse the victim and persuade them that he or she is wrong, over-reacting, is hysterical, is imagining things and generally that they are been mistaken. This repeated behaviour will eventually cause the victim to doubt the reality of what is before them and cause them to accept what the narcissist is telling him or her;

8. The cumulative effect of these abusive behaviours results in the victim losing their ability to think in a critical fashion, their self-confidence is lost, their self-worth is diminished and exhaustion, trauma and fear cause them to lose the ability to see the black flags at all or if they do, recognise what they mean and do something about it.

Accordingly, the black flags are often missed by victims, ignored or made to seem irrelevant. Understanding what these black flags are, what they mean and what will follow is crucial for anybody who is in a relationship, who is about to embark on seeking a relationship and especially for someone who may have already read **Red Flag: 50 Warning Signs of Narcissist Seduction** because there is a significant risk of being exposed to these black flags and failing to heed them. The consequence of doing so will be enormous and far-reaching for the victim.

I am in a position to note these black flags for you since I am a narcissist. I know what these black flags are, why they appear and what they signify. I do not detail this in a scientific fashion because that is the preserve of other people, but what I am able to do, is provide you with this information in a fashion and form which is usually unobtainable. There are many people who pronounce on my kind, but do so from the side-lines and have never experienced our corrosive touch. Victims of our behaviour naturally have experienced these black flags but may not know about them. We generate them and know what they signify and therefore my kind and I are in the best explain their significance to you. This amounts to an unrivalled opportunity for you, to guard against these abusive practices being used against you in the first place or for you to finally realise that it is happening to you and for you to then take steps to escape the abuse and protect yourself. There is no shame in failing to recognise them for the reasons that I have outlined above. This however is a premium opportunity for you to understand the nature of black flags and guard against them for you own well-being and that of the people who you love and care for.

If you have ever wondered "why did she do that?" or "why does he do this to me?" and been at a loss to understand, this book will take you to fifty ways in which this abuse manifests in day-to-day interactions, what form of abuse it actually and most of all why does the narcissistic abuser do it.

1. Loses Temper Over Nothing

You know this individual well. This person suddenly erupts in a rage which has come out of nowhere. They are not just angry, they are furious and this fury appears in the form of shouting, smashing things up, yelling abusive names and hitting people. It arrives from nowhere and is as shocking in the manner it manifests as it is in terms of how suddenly it appears. You may be having a normal conversation with a person and before you know it they have exploded. Their face is red, a drink is knocked over and they are ranting and raving at you. You have no idea why they have reacted like this. You do not recall saying anything that could have set them off. The red mist has descended and they prove nearly impossible to placate as the fury continues. You are dumbfounded and mystified as to why they have reacted in this manner. Sometimes you can see that they have reacted to some minor incident but their response is utterly disproportionate. On other occasions you have no idea at all what has triggered this tornado of rage.

This response tends to cause the following: -

- An analysis on the part of the person who is on the receiving end of this fury as they try and ascertain what it is that they have said which has upset the other person so much;

- Treading on egg-shells when dealing with the person to avoid a repetition of the outburst (this is a futile tactic);

- Repeated attempts to placate and please the person who has lost their temper

- Anxiety in the recipient;

Normal people do not lose their temper over nothing. Anger is a normal reaction to a number of stressors such as being placed in danger, threat to one's property or a threat to a person's loved one, an injustice, the loss of position, income or employment. Anger is an entirely normal reaction to events such as these. Invariably, where someone loses their temper for no reason or at the slightest provocation it is because their fury has been ignited.

We, as narcissists, have fury churning away at all times. It is waiting to be unleashed. See **Fury** for a more in-depth explanation of this dynamic between the victim and the narcissist. In essence, owing to our sense of entitlement, our sense of superiority and our belief that others are inferior to us we hate criticism. When we are criticised we are wounded by the comment so long as it is delivered in an unemotional fashion. If we are criticised as part of somebody shouting at us, this is providing us with fuel. We focus on the emotional response and not the content. In such a situation as that the criticism does not affect us in the same way. If, however the criticism is delivered in an unemotional way then it wounds us. It is worth pointing out that in many instances there is no actual criticism of us but it is this perception of being criticised that caused the problem. We look at the world in an entirely different way to you and consequently you may think you have said nothing that could be in anyway construed as a criticism. We will regard it differently. Once a criticism has been directed towards us then this churning fury is ignited. One of the ways that the fury ignites is as a rage and this is when we lash out at the person who has (often unwittingly) criticised us. The nature of this hot fury is such that it is beyond anger. It is unbridled and savage, resulting in abusive behaviour towards an innocent victim. That person will be on the receiving end of shouted insults, physical violence and see property damaged. The narcissist, when engaging in the heated fury which arises from the ignition of his or her fury, suffers a rage which blots out sound and vision. Words will not suffice in order to try and appear the furious narcissist. Visual cues such as a contrite expression, two hands raised with palms down and other signals of calming an apology are ignored as the enraged narcissist goes on the offensive. This offensive happens so that the recipient is upset, tearful, frightened or becomes angry. Any of these responses or others of an emotional nature are the required outcome from this outpouring of rage. This is because these emotional responses provide fuel to the narcissist. Fuel is our life blood and what we require from various people every day, especially those we are in an intimate relationship with. We need fuel in order to survive and we need fuel desperately and urgently when we have been wounded by criticism.

The ignition of fury results in somebody losing their temper on a thermonuclear scale (it can also cause cold fury or withdrawal but those are for different discussions – see **Fury**) and lashing out at that person who has apparently criticised the narcissist. This heated fury is savage, remorseless and abusive towards whoever is on the receiving end. It is unleashed because the narcissist has to defend him or herself to the perceived criticism and repair the wound. Fuel is needed to do that. Thus an emotional reaction must be obtained from the victim. Heated fury applied by way of an explosive temper is one method of getting that emotional reaction and thus the fuel.

Accordingly, if your partner or friend, colleague or brother loses his or her temper in a volcanic fashion without there being any reason for doing so, what you are suffering is abuse as a consequence of the narcissistic ignition of fury.

2. Cannot Take Criticism

Following on from the above, another indicator of an abusive characteristic pertinent to us as narcissists is our ability to take criticism. I mentioned above how our fury ignites when we are criticised. This is usually in the context of a perceived criticism. For example, if we are not invited to something (even when there was no reasonable reason to invite us – perhaps we had already explained we would be away) we regard this failure to invite us not as an understandable reaction to our expressed non-availability or even as an oversight, we will see it as a criticism of us. We are clearly not thought of as worth inviting. That is why we were not invited. That is a criticism of us.

Take another example. You place more food on my plate than you. I explode in a rage and you are mystified as to why. In my world you are suggesting that I eat too much and that I am fat (I know this seems ridiculous when looked at through your world view but not to us. We are special, brilliant and perfect and therefore we cannot be criticised in any fashion) and this suggestion is clearly a criticism and therefore my fury will ignite. If you placed less food on my plate than you then again I would explode with rage because now you are suggesting that you are entitled to more food than me and thus you must me more important than me and therefore that is another criticism. These and millions more are examples of where we will see a criticism (through our world view) where none actually exists (through your world view) or was even intended.

There is also the other issue whereby an actual criticism which is levelled at us cannot be accepted by us. The criticism may be entirely legitimate and may even be constructive in nature. If you told us that our report was helpful but it might have addressed the issue of poor sales in France in a more detailed fashion, we ignore the praise and focus on the criticism. How dare you suggest that our analysis was not correct? Who are you to be able to do that? You are inferior to me. You don't know half of what I know. I do not regard your opinion (save as to when it is praising me) as having any validity. If we are having a golf lesson and the instructor tries to recommend a change in our swing, even though he is trying to help us, we regard this as a criticism. In such instances, where the criticism is overt rather than perceived our response is less likely to appear as heated fury. In such instances it will be cold fury (namely not speaking to someone) or withdrawal, in order to get away from the source of the criticism. Once again just walking off and leaving someone is abusive behaviour. It is regarded as ill-mannered and impolite. It will happen anywhere. At a party, in a shopping centre at a church. If we can withdraw we will do so as we slink away and seek refuge to recover from the wound caused by this overt criticism. The consequence is that the narcissist may develop a reputation for being stroppy or haughty with people, but the reality is that the reaction to this overt criticism is either giving the cold shoulder to someone or walking off. Neither of these reactions is pleasant to endure and especially so if the person who made the criticism (no matter how well-intended) is in a position where other people witness this response. They are left feeling foolish as we stride out of the room or stand there glowering and saying nothing. As with the reactions detailed in the first instance above, this repeated behaviour will result in: -

- Anxiety for the recipient;
- The need to placate or please the narcissist;
- The need to make excuses for the narcissist's behaviour when in a setting where other people are present, which is often awkward and embarrassing;
- The person making the comment suffering from being controlled. They will second guess the narcissist's response and end up walking on egg shells as they check every they say in order to avoid causing the situation to arise again.

If someone cannot take criticism and reacts with silent treatment or withdrawal, then this is abusive behaviour. Silent treatment is an abusive behaviour in itself and is one which is often favoured by our kind to belittle and upset the target, again for the purposes of exerting control and drawing fuel from the victim as they try to break the silence and find out what is wrong. One of the manifestations of this silent treatment is in the context of someone who is unable to accept criticism, no matter how legitimate, constructive or well-intentioned that criticism is. We are above any form of criticism and when it happens we are wounded, we have to respond to this wounding and we do so, especially with overt criticism through cold fury or withdrawal.

3. Makes Going out a Battle

Many victims of a narcissistic abuser will have experienced the battle of going out. Over time the victim will come to dread having to mention a forthcoming social engagement which does not involve us. Firstly, the mention of something which we are not a part of will be regarded as a criticism so the victim will suffer one of the reactions mentioned in the first two chapters above. It does not matter if it is an event to which we would not be invited or could even attend. We will regard our non-inclusion as a criticism and erupt accordingly. Once that has been dealt with, when the actual event comes around, we will cause a scene, be nasty to the person who is going out and make them feel awful for attending, hopefully resulting in them deciding against going.

We do not like you to socialise without us. Why would you want to be anywhere other than by our side marvelling at how brilliant we are? Why on earth would you want to spend time with someone who is clearly inferior to us? What are you up to by going out with someone else? You are clearly being disloyal and that does not please us. Moreover, you are not providing us with any fuel by asserting some form of independence and that is a terrible and selfish thing for you to do. We do not like you to spend time with other people since we fear that they exert some malign influence over you. We know they will be trying to undermine us in your eyes and turn you against us. We know it is because they are jealous of what we have together and rather than be pleased for you, they are smearing my good name. You want to listen to them as well don't you, otherwise why would you be going?

Our careful and structured control of you, our calculated isolation of you, all stand to be damaged by your socialising with those who we have not control over.

This is why we make it such a battle if you are going socialising without us. In our world there are several reasons why this should not happen, we lose fuel, our control over you might be weakened, we may be criticised and therefore we need to respond in an unpleasant way to prevent you from going out. If we are not able to prevent your attendance we will do all we can beforehand to make you feel guilty and so you are on edge, anxious and unable to enjoy the event once you are there. We try hard so far to prevent you from going but for some reason there are two or three of your friends who proved immune to our charm and have organised to go out with you and we are not invited. You are determined to go. I should feel sorry for them since they are selfish, bitter and twisted, but I don't feel sorry for them because I don't feel sorry do I, only for myself. I want you with me, where I can keep an eye on you and control you. I want you here where you are supplying me with fuel. This is your rightful place and by organising to go out for your meal with these friends you are telling me that I am not good enough to spend time with. You are criticising me and that wounds me. I have to stop you wounding me. I have to stop you going. I have to maintain the upper hand. Thus because of your selfish behaviour the Battle of Going Out is joined. Despite my attempts to prevent you going so far, I will continue right up until the moment you leave the house. I detail below a typical exchange that will take place when this happens.

"You never said that you were going out," I begin as I see you getting ready in the bathroom. You halt applying your make-up and turn to me.

"Yes I did, I told you last week and again this morning."

"No you didn't."

"Yes I did, I remember."

"No you did not. I would have remembered if you had told me," I answer.

" I put it on the calendar." You walk to the kitchen and return holding a calendar with the words 'Girls meal out - Leonardo's'.

"See?" you ask and jab a finger at the words.

"That? I thought that was referring to your nieces, not you, you never said."

"Seriously? Come on, why would my nieces be going to Leonardo's on their own?" you ask.

"You've just written that in when you were fetching the calendar. Look, the ink is still drying."

You sigh in exasperation.

"I told you about it, it is in the calendar. I have not been out in weeks."

"Well neither have I," I comment.

"What? You were out last Friday," you answer voice rising.

"That was with work."

"It was still going out," you reply.

"That is not the same. You know I have to schmooze clients; it is hardly pleasure. I have to do that for business reasons so I think you are being unfair by saying that is a night out for me."

"Those clients you were out with are your friends, it was a right piss up."

"Oh sorry, I forgot, you were there weren't you, you know all about how I conduct my business don't you?" I declare.

"No I don't but they are your friends."

"So I am not allowed to have clients who are friends now am I? Jesus, why don't you just stop me from having any friends at all eh? Why not stop me going anywhere? You would like that wouldn't you? Just having me stuck in here all the time."

"What are you talking about, I let you do as you please."

"No you don't. You are determined to keep me on a leash. My friends take the piss out of me for how little time I get to spend with them."

You halt your application of the lipstick.

"Who has said that?"

"Several people. Jim, Richard and John. They say I am under the thumb."

"Huh, they have a cheek, Jim is completely under the thumb of Jessica."

"No he's not, but you just change the subject why don't you. You should be staying in with me you never want to do that anymore."

"Don't be silly, I am with you most of the time. Look it is just an informal meal with a few of my friends, it is no big deal."

"If it is not important then why do you have to go?"

"Because I want to," you answer.

"Where are you going?"

"You know that, I am going to Leonardo's."

"Really? Who with?"

"Jane, Sarah, Mary and Stephanie, oh and Carrie."

"I don't believe you, you have just made that up."

"What? No I haven't."

"You are meeting a man aren't you? Come on who is it?"

"No you are being stupid."

"Don't call me stupid. I am not the one going out and leaving their other half on their own," I begin to shout and you jolt at the sudden change in volume.

"You are up to something; you have a different perfume on. Who is he?"

"Seriously, you are paranoid, I am meeting the girls."

"No I am not, who do you think you are saying that to me, you are messing around. I know you are. You have been acting strangely the last few weeks. I know you are. Admit it," I move towards you and stand over you barking into your face. You back away, eyes widening fearfully.

"I haven't, honestly, I haven't."

"I should let you go anyway you whore. I don't know I bother with you. I was planning a pleasant evening in for us. I was going to cook you your favourite and I have a delicious bottle of Chablis chilling but as usual you are being selfish."

"Please don't shout at me, I am just going out with my friends, I am allowed to have some friends aren't I?"

"Not those harpies, they have it in for me, I hate them. I hate you."

"Oh please don't be like that, look I will be back by ten at the latest so we can still have some time together," you suggest.

"Is that supposed to make me feel pleased? Why would I want to spend time with you, you are a slut? I see, you want to have your way with him and then rub it in my face. You are such a bitch."

You have backed away from my tirade, wincing with each bellowed sentence. This allows me to snatch up your clutch bag.

"You can't go out with no keys and no money," I say holding the bag aloft.

"Please I only want to see my friends, I rarely see them as it is, please give me my bag back, why are you being so horrible?"

"Because you are cheating on me. I am not having you spend our money on some other man."

"There is no other man, how many times do I have to tell you? Please let me go."

"No. You are not going. You are staying here with me."

"I can't cancel, not this late," you say in dejection.

"Of course you can. He does not matter."

"There is no he. It is the girls."

"So you say. You are not going. If you do that is me and you finished."

"What, just because I want to see my friends?" You slump on to the bed, shoulders hunched and your head in your hands.

"You don't need them you have got me."

"Why does it always have to be like this, every time I try and do something you do this," you protest and your voice breaks with the first sob of frustration.

"No I don't stop trying to blame me when you are at fault," I growl.

"You always do this, make feel guilty or do something to stop me going out."

"Rubbish, you are making things up again. You are just trying to make me feel bad for you. It won't work you know that."

You begin crying as I stand power surging through me.

"Here," I order as I pull your phone from your bag and throw it down on the bed besides you, " ring them and tell them you can't make it, say you don't feel well or something. I will pour the Chablis."

Still sobbing you fumble for the phone and pick it up before dialling the number. I stand triumphant drinking deep of the fuel you have given me during this exchange. I have won the battle once again and this time I did not even have to escalate it like I did last time. I suppose that was just as well really seeing as how you had only just replaced those mirrors I smashed.

In such an instance you are witnessing several different narcissistic manipulations in play – triangulation, guilt, blame-shifting and projection. This is what those terms look like when applied to a real situation. The outcome is abusive. You are shouted at, you are controlled, your independence is curtailed and you are disrespected as an individual in your own right. This is because we do not regard you as a separate person. We consider you as an appliance that is attached to us. You are to provide fuel and do as we want. You are not to rebel or put yourself in situations where our control is eroded or nullified.

We know in your mind that going out is harmless. You want to see a show, spend time with your friends and enjoy yourself. You want to go and do something different and then hopefully come back and enjoy discussing it with your partner. You might achieve that with someone normal and healthy but you will not when it is us. Another way this abusive behaviour manifests is detailed below as I describe an alternative method of ruining your night out, yet again because I do not want you doing something without me which undermines me.

The issue of going out also presents me with opportunities to reinforce who is in charge in this relationship. It allows me to undermine you, disappoint you and control you and invariably, as with everything that I do, fuel will flow.

A typical instance of this occurring might involve one of our kind receiving a call from you during the course of the afternoon.

"Hi, how are you?" you ask pleasantly.

"Busy, busy what is it?"

"I am just reminding you that I am going out tonight, okay?"

"And?"

"Well I did not want you forgetting like you did last time."

"I did not forget; you just didn't tell me about it."

"Well look I am not getting into all of that now, that was last time. I just wanted to make sure that you will be home by 6pm as I need to be there by 7pm and I need you to look after the kids whilst I get ready."

"Can't your mother look after them or something?"

"No they are out and anyway, Michael is not well. He has been off school all day and I don't want a casual childminder looking after him, I want it to be you or me."

"Well if he is that ill perhaps you should cancel your plans?"

"No. I am not going to. I do not have to because you are available to watch him. In any event, even if I wanted to cancel I cannot. I can't let my friends down, this is an important occasion."

"Are you sure there isn't somebody who can look after Michael, I wanted to go to the bar this evening, we have completed a major deal here."

"No. My sister is out of town and the only other people are neighbours and registered childminders and it is not fair asking non-family when one of the kids is ill. I don't like it. It has to be mum or dad looking after them."

"Okay, okay I get it, it has to be one of us."

"Yes and it is going to be you because I am going out. Okay?"

"Sure, fine 6pm you say?"

"Yes."

"Right."

6pm arrives and I am sat in the bar explaining how I brought the deal to the business and I saw it through. Several junior colleagues are listening intently seeking to curry favour with me. I am sat on my throne, my subjects paying homage. I glance at my watch and order champagne to toast the deal. The evening is just getting started and I have my eye on a pretty accountant who I have not seen before.

I feel my 'phone vibrate and pull it from my jacket pocket. Your name is on the display. I smile and let it slip back into the pocket as I pay for the champagne and begin pouring it for those assembled with me. I feel the 'phone ring again and stop. I continue my conversation and feel a succession of vibrations as a few messages land. During a lull between my anecdotes I wander over to the toilet and whilst there I check my phone. There are three messages from you.

"Hi, I hope you are on your way. Call me please xxx"

"Where are you? I am trying to get ready."

"This is totally unfair. Where the hell are you?"

The fuel hits and power surges through me as I feel the frustration from those messages and picture you pacing through the house trying to get ready as you are subjected to the demands from the children. I do not turn my phone off, I am ready for further vibrations and messages as I look in the mirror, smooth my hair and give myself a winning smile.

"Think you can tell me to be a childminder do you?" I ask the mirror.

"Nobody stops me from going out."

I return to the bar and grab my champagne flute as my phone goes again. I do not even bother to look to see who is calling as I know and the power rises inside. As I begin to talk to the pretty accountant I savour the fuel that will be coming my way. The looks and words of admiration from the beautiful bean counter all the while my mobile 'phone buzzes and vibrates away like a trapped wasp, conveying to me your anger and annoyance at being kept at home. I know, empathic person that you are, that you will not put an evening out ahead of your ill child and once again you will martyr yourself. I know from our earlier conversation that there is no prospect of you calling someone else in as a child minder and you will be left at home alternating between crying and calling me all the names under the sun. Knowing that I have been able to do what I want whilst keeping you at home underlines my dominance and affirms why I am the superior one. Your repeated messages and telephone calls just feed me more fuel as once again I win this battle. I sometimes wonder why you even bother but I am glad you do, after all, I need the fuel from your reaction to my control.

If you actually manage to make it out, you will no escape unscathed. You may find we invent some kind of emergency to force you to come home, we may bombard you with messages so you feel uncomfortable and cannot enjoy yourself. Each time the 'phone buzzes you feel a sick sensation as you anticipate another abusive message which will just be foreshadowing the treatment you will get once you get home. You wish that you had just stayed at home as it is not worth the aggravation and the horrible treatment. All you want to do is go out. Is that such a crime? Yes, in our skewed world it is.

When your taxi halts outside after you have managed to escape the house for a rare night out and you pay the driver, eyes flitting back and forth from that ajar door, the gateway to hell that has yawned open and is beckoning you in, your despair and apprehension rises. The outside world has no comprehension of what goes on between those walls. To everyone else we appear a content couple, enjoying a good lifestyle. Our carefully constructed façade ensures that we are afforded the recognition and status that our kind is entitled to. We ensure that everyone else knows us to be capable, successful, entertaining and personable.

The drive home or the taxi journey seems to take an age and you can feel our churning fury as you anticipate what is to come once you get home. As you round the corner and the house comes into view you want to pass out, you want to be removed from the situation but you know you cannot. You walk with heavy footsteps towards that door. We saw you approaching and left the door open, in the way we do when you have gone out without us. It is a clear signal. You are entering our domain now and you will answer for your lack of loyalty in going out. The list of transgressions, both real and imagined, is long and we will always find something that you have done incorrectly during your time away from the house and once returned you will be punished as we unleash one of our manipulative tools from our devil's toolkit in order to devalue you. We hope you might argue back and unleash some anger, but more often than not as we push the front door closed with a click and move towards you it is the upset and tears that flow. As our shadow falls over you, already your eyes are welling with tears as you know what will come behind that closed door.

We will try to stop you going out, we will try to get you to come back early, we will make the evening unpleasant if you have managed to go out and you will dread our welcome when you return. Other abusive behaviours such as shouting, silent treatments, violence and so forth will be used, but the fact of us controlling you in this way concerning your own separate social life is an abusive form in itself. It is designed to achieve the following: -

- Cause you to give us fuel;

- Control you;

- Bind you to us;

- Over-compensate in other ways to try and please us

- Make you less like to want to go out next time, because it just is not worth the aggravation;

- Reduce your independence;

- Erode your sense of self

- Assert that we own you and you are part of us.

No matter how pleasantly the explanation might initially be,

"Oh I want us to stay in and do something together."

"I don't like you going into town without me, I worry you might get hurt."

"I miss you when you go, I want you stay with me please?"

The nasty and unpleasant elements of this form of abuse will show. Your social life should not be an issue but we will make it so. That is a black flag of abuse.

4. Infidelity

Infidelity is a given when you are ensnared by one of our kind. We know that it is not pleasant for you to think of us in the arms of another, conjoined in sexual congress as we do things with them that we have done with you and then we return to you. We know that infidelity is something that someone like you abhors. You have a strong moral compass, you behave in an honest and decent fashion and expect us to do the same. That will not happen. You place considerable belief in the question of trust and the concept of monogamy. Our infidelity will manifest in lots of different ways: -

- Having sexual liaisons with third parties, some of whom will be strangers and others will be prospects who are looking to seduce;
- Sending and receiving text messages of a sexual content;
- Describing online what we want to do to someone and they to you;
- Sexual liaisons with your friends and family members;

Although I know it is scant consolation to you since ultimately it is the breach of trust which causes you the greatest pain, we do not commit acts of infidelity because we want the sex. Admittedly, the physical sensation is enjoyable but that is not the reason we are repeatedly unfaithful. In terms of our attitudes to sex and especially sex with you, read **Sex and the Narcissist**. For the purposes of this publication it is sufficient to explain that when are unfaithful the sex is not the primary purpose. It is the fact that in your world sex is equated with love, affection and attraction and as a consequence it serves a purpose as a formidable weapon in our hands. We use it to seduce to we can additional fuel from third parties. We use it to seduce a new prospect who will provide us with fuel and will ultimately replace you. Initially we will be covert about our infidelity as we do not wish to damage having you as our primary source and therefore our need to obtain fuel from secondary sources through infidelity will remain covered up. Over time we will continue to use sex with other people as a means of gaining additional fuel but we will also be doing this to seduce your replacement. Eventually when we start our devaluation of you, we will be far less covert concerning our extra-marital affairs and often we will not care if you know or not. Indeed, we may even flaunt a mistress in front of you for the purposes of making you try harder and to provoke you so that you provide us with additional negative fuel.

Infidelity is not about the sex. It is about fuel. It is about control. Being unfaithful to you abuses your trust, it pours scorn on the vows we have taken and makes a mockery of you and what you stand for. It is abusive behaviour and to expect a narcissist to always be faithful is like expecting the tide to stop advancing when you tell it do so. It just will not happen. Infidelity is second nature to us because the weapon that is sex is just too good not to use to gain additional fuel. If there was another device that was so potent we would use it instead. The fact that sex feels enjoyable is just a matter of nerve endings and a pleasant side-effect. For us, sex is all about using it to further our aims; gathering fuel.

We will be unfaithful to you at some point. That is a guarantee. When we are first seducing you, we will be in the process of devaluing someone else leading to his or her discard. We most likely will have withdrawn sex from the victim who we are devaluing and be having sex with you as the new object of our seduction. This does not mean that since you are the apple of our eye we will be faithful to you. We will have intermittent sex with the person who is subjected to the devaluation either as a means of giving them a short golden period again or for the purposes of extracting further fuel by subjecting them to humiliating sexual activities. We will also be courting other prospects also as well as you and therefore there is a strong likelihood we will be bedding that person also. We will, when seducing you, maintain an image of fidelity since that is what you expect. If you are conducting an affair with us, we will assure you that our current partner (whom we are devaluing) never has sex with us, we sleep in separate beds and so on. We will bemoan the fact they never have sex with us in order to draw sympathy from you as the new prospect.

By contrast, we will triangulate you as the new prospect with our current partner. We will drop heavy hints that we are being unfaithful or even actively admit it in order to further the hurt. Our rationale behind this is that monogamy is for the little people and this does not include us. That would make us less special and we cannot have that. We are entitled to seek sex outside of a relationship because this is our inalienable right to enable us to obtain fuel. We feel no guilt in doing this, we do not respect any vows we may have given to remain faithful to you and we have no qualms about coupling with someone else. The reason for this is that we have to do it and in a perverse way, the only reflection on you is that you are not giving us the fuel we need. It is not a reaction to what you look like, what you do, who your friends are or what your interests might happen to be. We will of course use them, as a method of lashing out at you should you try and question us about our infidelity because as I have explained in **Manipulated** we will deploy blame shifting frequently when we are under attack. It is often the case that when a partner learns of the infidelity of their partner that they will scrutinise their own conduct.

"Is it something I have done?"

This means that you will examine your own behaviour and try to improve in some way because you will want to salvage our relationship. The fact of your addiction means you do not want to let us go. You will be mightily hurt and offended by our infidelity but you will try to find some way of fixing it because that is what you like to do. If our infidelity shows any risk of causing you to depart, we will hastily reinstate the golden period, as a Preventative Hoover, if you will, to stop you departing from us. Most of the time however, because of the way you are, you blame yourselves (often because we warp your way of thinking to do this) and you try to patch things over. Your need to resolve matters results in you clinging to us notwithstanding our fidelity. Indeed, in some instances you want to prove that you are better than the person we committed our infidelity with. You want to fight to retain us and ensure that our relationship triumphs.

We will also use infidelity as a means by which to control you and make you do what we want: -

"If you gave me more attention I would not go elsewhere."

"If you put out more often I would not have to get it from someone else."

"Perhaps if you hadn't let yourself slide I wouldn't stray would I?"

"If you thought more about me rather than yourself perhaps it would not have happened?"

"I won't leave you, I should, but I will stay but some things are going to have to change."

You are the victim. We have committed the transgression but other than when we fear you might leave us and sever our supply of fuel, we will not apologise but pin the blame on you. You will have been subjected to a succession of manipulation wiles in order to browbeat you and lower your resistance so that when we unveil our infidelity we use it as a method of getting what we want from you, namely more fuel and more control.

Infidelity is bad enough in the context of a "normal" relationship. With our kind it will always happen, it will always happen with many people and will do so repeatedly. It is a further black flag of abusive behaviour.

5. Disappears

If you find that your intimate partner has a habit of disappearing without notice and is then difficult or impossible to contact, you are dealing with a further form of abuse. This is another manifestation of the silent treatment. Ordinarily silent treatment falls into two distinct categories: -

- We do not speak to you but remain physically proximate to you. We will speak to other people but not you. We may completely ignore you or glare at you whilst not speaking;

- We remove ourselves from your presence. We do not contact you and make ourselves uncontactable. We will not answer the 'phone (we may even change numbers of block you). We will not respond to e-mails and texts (again possibly blocking) and we will not answer the door to you if we live somewhere else. If we live with you we may seek sanctuary (in our minds) in a bolthole (see more below) which could be a house we have kept on, a friend's place, the office or a hotel room.

I am referring to the second form of the silent treatment. This is known as the absent silent treatment. Its duration varies. We may absent ourselves for half an hour but be utterly incommunicado during that period. We will ensure you know that we are implementing a silent treatment as we will just walk out. In other instances, where the absent silent treatment is for longer, we will give you no warning. You will suddenly find you cannot locate us or contact us. This might be a day or it could run to weeks. It is as if we have walked off the face of the planet. We will utilise our coterie of supporters and our Lieutenants to keep you at bay, to throw you off the scent in terms of finding us and frustrating any method of contacting us. Why do we do this?

- Draw fuel from you. We read your messages, we see the phone lighting up as you keep calling. We know you will be upset, worried, angry and so on and this provides us with fuel. We do not even have to witness your emotional state. Knowing that is how you will react to this vanishing act is all we need.
- Create a state of anxiety for you as you do not know what is happening;
- Exert control over you. You keep trying to contact us and you worry what has happened. You wonder what is wrong and what you have done.
- To tell you that you are worthless. Would a healthy person behave in this manner in respect of somebody they loved? No they would not. They love and care about the other person. They may sometimes need some space but they would explain that to be the case and keep in touch. We just vanish because we want to send you a clear signal that you do not matter to us, if you did, we would not do this would we?
- Punishment for some transgression on your part, either real or imagined.

As I mentioned, in many cases we will execute our disappearing act through the use of a bolthole. The bolthole is a very important location to my kind. It can come in many forms but the message it sends to you is very clear; you are not welcome. Our kind must always have a bolthole to which we can retreat. This is our sacred territory where you are not allowed to venture. When we first engage with you, you should notice two things which invariably occur. We will spend most of our time where you live. This enables us to stay by your side as often as we can in order to continue our seduction of you. It also means that your resources are the ones that are used up. It is your food, your cable bill and your utilities that we use and since it is your home we will not contribute to those bills. If asked, we will point out that we have our own overheads to cover although of course they will be reduced as we are rarely there. We stay at your house and ensure that you provide us with a set of keys so that we may come and go. You are invariably not given a set for our house. When we decide that we want to engage in our methods of gathering fuel and/or we decide to subject you to a period of the effective silent treatment, we return to our house. You cannot enter and we are able to watch you pleading and begging from through a gap in the curtains as you turn up wanting to see us as you try to work out why we have just disappeared.

On the occasions we do allow you to stay at our property then this is little more than a licence which is revocable on a moment's notice. If we want you out of our space then we will turf you out, irrespective of time, weather or convenience. We like to do this to reinforce that it is us who are in control in this relationship and not you.

Even if we properly move in together at one property or buy another one together, we shall manipulate the situation so that your house is sold and the proceeds used towards the joint property whilst we keep our house on. You will be puzzled by such a move but we will find an excuse to do this.

"It represents a useful investment opportunity so I am going to keep it."

"Now is now the right time to sell in that area."

"I need a pied a terre for when I work late in the city."

"I want the market to pick up first before I consider selling the property."

"I don't want to sell it because my ex-wife will come sniffing around for a share of it."

We will find the reason not to sell it. This is of course not the real reason. We want to keep it as our bolthole. We might decide to provide you with a set of keys for this property but then when you try to use them to go inside to find us, the door is bolted so you cannot access the property. Your shouts of frustration prove to be delicious fuel as we sit and listen to you.

Sometimes we will use hotel rooms as boltholes or the office or a bar. As long as it somewhere to which we can retreat and have you guessing as to where we have gone as you frantically telephone and text us, then it serves its purpose.

If there is not another property that we can go to, we will create a bolthole within the house that we share with you. The study will have a lock fitted and we keep the key on our person all the time. It may be a man-cave in the basement or the garden shed, but there is one simple rule concerning this bolthole. It may be in or around our joint property but you are not to enter it ever. We regard this as our throne room where we sit and plot our schemes. The chosen few will be admitted in order to emphasise to you how you are not special enough to be allowed in and thus prompt a reaction from you. We know it will drive you crazy wondering what we are doing in this place, especially if our guests are of the opposite sex. We will spend hours in this place, secreted away, often sleeping there too. We may spend days as we enforce an absent silent treatment under your nose. Here we can send our messages and engage in our telephone calls with other sources of fuel, free from interference yet still gaining fuel from you as we know you will be in a spin thinking about what we are doing. We can enter the chat rooms, work our way through the dating sites and blitz social media, all entrenched in our control room. We will delight in sending you a message compelling you to bring us food or a drink and leave it at the door. You of course will comply in order to try and sneak a glimpse of what is going on inside or to try and talk to us, yet the door will be pushed closed in your face.

On occasions the bolt hole will be temporary in nature. Should we decide that we wish to exercise some withdrawal late at night when you are expecting intimacy and love-making, we will move to sleep in the spare room, sliding across the lock we had fitted. We will lie there smiling as we hear you tapping on the door and sobbing for us to come back to the shared bed.

The bolthole is very important to us. It allows us a clear way of reinforcing our control and superiority, it provides a base from which we can engage in our schemes and plotting and it is crucial in the implementation of silent treatment.

If you realise that the person you have a relationship with creates and uses boltholes there is every chance that he or she is one of us.

Once the absent silent treatment is over (and there will be no logical reason to you as to why it has ended) we will return and act as if nothing has changed or that nothing has happened. We may make up excuses such as needed to recharge our batteries, or needing some "me time" or having to put some things into perspective. We may even look to draw some more fuel. You will undoubtedly be relieved that we have come back and this will provide us with fuel, but if you start to question us too much about why we did it, where we have been and what we have been doing and we will go on the attack and blame you, stating you were the reason why we had to be alone and we will do this to provoke another reaction in you to gain fuel.

Should you find that someone you have a relationship with, particularly an intimate partner, keeps engaging in disappearing acts you are not dealing with someone who needs space and time-out. They are abusing you through their disappearances and this is yet another black flag of abuse.

6. Sings the Praises of Hated Exes

Nearly everyone has an ex. Ex-girlfriend from school, an ex-boyfriend from college, an ex-partner or ex-spouse. We all accumulate them although we have more than most as we go through relationships like a donkey eats strawberries. The ex will crop up in conversation in the context of a new relationship. Some people will only give their ex a passing comment, preferring not to dwell on the past and certainly not to do so with a new person they are interested in. Others may explain who they are on good terms and occasionally bump into one another, they may be civil with one another owing to the existence of children or they may refer to their ex as being not a bad person but it just did not work out. Other people may refer to their ex as something of a nightmare and give an explanation but do not labour the point. Most people either want to remain on good terms but if that is not possible then they prefer to not dwell on what has happened and move on. We don't.

It is universal amongst our kind that we will talk about our immediate ex (and most likely the ones before that) in terms of how awful they were, how we tried and did everything to please them and that the ex was abusive towards us. We will provide you with a catalogue of horrors concerning their apparent behaviour most of which will be fabricated and the rest will be exaggerated and taken out of context. We do this for three reasons: -

- To make you feel sorry for us and want to care for us, thus binding you closer to us;
- So you provide us with fuel by being sympathetic and/or telling us that we are a good person and deserve better; and
- To make you dislike and be wary of your predecessor when he or she tries to tell you the truth of what happened between us.

36

We are vociferous in our hatred of this individual. We will provide you with considerable detail about how terribly they behaved towards us whilst telling you all about the things that we did for them and how we got no thanks for it. This is a classic projection on our part. This stance is maintained during our seduction of you and is a red flag.

Should you then notice that your partner is referring to your predecessor in favourable and complimentary terms such as: -

"I miss her cooking; she was a really good cook."

"Cheryl would not have spoken to me like you just did, she always treated me with respect."

"I wish you kept the house tidier. Hilary was very domesticated; you could learn a few things from her."

"I tell you something, Donna was not frigid like you, she was always up for it. Maybe I should hook up with her again?"

Then this is a black flag and is a manifestation of triangulation and our legendary hypocrisy. You will be subjected to frequent comparisons with your predecessor. We will talk about them in glowing terms with a wistful look in our eye. We will make noises about contacting them. If you point out that we said this person was abusive and horrible you will be met with more manipulations in the form of denial, deflection and projection.

"I never said that about her. Why do you have to lie all the time?"

"I only said it because I knew you would be jealous otherwise. You are always jealous of me being friendly with other women."

"You said those things about him, not me."

"I cannot believe you are accusing me of saying such things. Why would I invent something like that? You are sick, there is something wrong with you, you need to get some help."

This volte face is extraordinary to you. Why do we do this?

- When we are devaluing you, we need to take steps that provoke negative reactions from you. Referring to the once hated and despised ex in this fashion causes you to react in several ways. You are confused by it and bewildered. You may feel threatened and double your efforts to please me. You may be jealous and react accordingly. In whichever case we gain fuel.
- We exert control over you by making you feel that your position with us is under threat.
- We wish to punish you for the decrease in positive fuel.
- We want to hoover the predecessor to obtain some delicious hoover fuel and therefore we begin to think of them in complimentary terms. This contradictory stance is evident to you but entirely acceptable to us. Your predecessor served no purpose as an appliance, after a time and was thus discarded. We hated them for failing us. We wanted you instead. You were marvellous but now you are not. The predecessor will give us hoover fuel so in our world they are marvellous again. We are able to shift these stances without any concern because they provide us with what we want, namely fuel.

This confusing, unsettling and contradictory behaviour is abusive as it will set you on edge, it will have you trying to convince us that we once said the other person was horrible and it will begin to cause you to doubt yourself as to what was actually said. It provides us with the means to degrade you and reinforce our view of you as a liar and a troublemaker by projecting on to you. It makes no sense to you and rather than see it for what it is, a black flag of abuse, you will try and rationalise it and understand what it is that you have done or why we have changed our minds. You will try to do this by looking at it through your world view and therefore you will be unable to make sense of it. The confusion continues and the tolls exacted from you increases.

7. Refusal to Undertake Menial Chores

We may have engaged in undertaking tasks such as stacking the dishwasher, helping with the laundry, taking the rubbish out and tidying up. We did not want to do this because it is not something that someone as brilliant and elevated as us should have to do. We are not a minion. We may however do it purely for the purpose of appearances so you think that we are domesticated, helpful and willing to pull our weight for the purposes of the relationship. We will keep this up during the seduction period and then it will halt. We know that it is expected in a relationship that there is a division of labour, a sharing of responsibilities when we live together but we do not regard that as a proper reflection of status. We are more important than you, you are there to serve us. Accordingly, we should not even be expected to carry out menial chores, never mind do them, by reason of our status. By comparison, you should be undertaking these chores for us.

This behaviour is a form of abuse because: -

- It demeans you;
- It shows that we hold you in contempt;
- We expect you to do everything for us as a matter of right;
- This will often over burden you (given other responsibilities that you have)

Why do we do this?

- We assist to begin with as I have explained in order to make you think that we are a helpful and kind person so you are drawn to us. Like many of our manipulations we give you something and do so in spades so you become used to it, love it, rely on it and become addicted to it. I am not suggesting you become addicted to us helping out with menial chores but you will welcome it and to an extent expect us to pull our weight. The effect of removing it becomes more powerful;

- By withdrawing any help that we once provided this confuses you and causes you to question why this has happened. You will ask us and do so in a puzzled and frustrated manner (thus giving us fuel) and then start to question your own conduct;

- By withdrawing any help, we once provided we reinforce the perception that you a worth less than us;

- You provide us with fuel by virtue of your reactions. Firstly, to the withdrawal and then the fact that we will not do things to help. You become upset, frustrated and angry;

- Your pleas for assistance and moaning at us for not doing so provides us with a further opportunity to draw fuel by criticising you for expecting us to help out ("I am at work all day supporting this household and you expect me to come back and start cleaning up? "Leave aside the fact you hold down a job as well.) and for creating arguments which will draw more fuel;

- By burdening you we will tire you out and therefore you will be less able to resist our other forms on manipulation;

- We expect to be waited on hand and foot. We have a huge sense of entitlement, regard ourselves as superior and therefore this is the way it should be. We will see no hypocrisy in having once helped and that we no longer do. That was then and this is now. Different circumstances dictated by our needs applied.

- Our energy must be conserved for the acquisition of fuel, not the cleaning of shoes and mowing the lawn.

- If we are a Victim Narcissist we will use one of our many ailments as an explanation for why we cannot help out.

This refusal to assist with menial chores is nothing to do with laziness. We are industrious creatures when it comes to gathering fuel and extending our machinations over our victims, so do not think that it is a symptom of laziness. It is purely a further method of abusive manipulation.

are the life raft that can save you when in actual fact we are the very instrument which is making matters worse for you. This is how insidious and dangerous we are.

Thus having established that devaluation will happen and a brief explanation as to why this is, what is the role of sex in this devaluation? Why do we use sex as a weapon when we are devaluing you? In a similar vein to its use during seduction, it is all about gathering fuel from you (although this time of a negative variety) and controlling you.

During devaluation sex will primarily be used in two ways: -

- It is removed because we regard you as sexless; and
- When we do engage in it is used as a tool to devalue you

When you have failed in your obligation to provide us with fuel and devaluation starts, your sexual attraction which was a means of gathering positive fuel also wanes. We begin to regard you as sexless. In certain situations, this means that sex is completely withdrawn and sexual engagement occurs with other people. This is in effect a manifestation of the Madonna/whore complex which I address in greater detail in **Sex and the Narcissist**.

In other situations, there will be a withdrawal of sex but not totally as the sexual arena will be used purely for the purpose of devaluation because the negative fuel to be gathered is so enticing. The Victim Variety of narcissist is most likely to withdraw sex altogether owing to his stance as being largely uninterested in it but also because the attraction of his primary care giver as the Madonna appeals to him particularly. The cerebral narcissist will shift the emphasis by engaging in verbally humiliating sexual behaviour in order to gather fuel, whilst largely abstaining from the physical act. Somatic and elite narcissists are less prone to complete withdrawal as they see the sexual act as still available to them for the purposes of gathering fuel through devaluation.

The use of sex during the devaluation stage is a dark place where the most intimate act is used against you repeatedly. There are many ways of using sex as a weapon, the arsenal that can be used against you is extensive. I detail below some of the more common methods of using sex as a weapon during devaluation in order to abuse you.

- Denying orgasm
- Rape
- We no longer initiate sex
- When you try and initiate sex we reject you
- We deliberately talk about other women to raise the suggestion in your mind that we are having sex with them and not you
- We watch pornography (more on this later) in order to show we are interested in sex but just not with you
- We will turn our back on you in bed
- Our use of prostitutes
- We will sleep in the spare room or on the sofa to be away from you and the usual arena of sex
- We will accuse you of being a nymphomaniac and not caring about feelings, the fact we are tired from working so hard to support you and the family etc.
- We will accuse you of having affairs to legitimise our withdrawal of sexual interest in you
- We will accuse you of dressing like a slut so that you do not appeal to us

- Ridicule your performance in bed by suggesting you are useless (despite the many compliments we will have showered you with previously, which only adds to your hurt and confusion)
- Indulging in group sex and/or making you do so
- Denying we like something that we once proclaimed to love doing with you
- Triangulating you with past lovers by praising their sexual performances and telling you how she would do x and y better than you
- Triangulating you with a current lover by praising their sexual performances
- Calling you frigid despite there being evidence to the contrary
- Insistence on our orgasm
- Calling you sluttish and a nymphomaniac despite evidence to the contrary
- Labelling you as homosexual when you are not and vice versa
- Expressing our view that we are actually homosexual because sex with you has horrified us and left us scarred
- Mocking you by saying your breasts are too small or too large or similar comments concerning physical sexual appearance
- Bondage
- Use of degrading names whilst engaged in sexual intercourse

- Forced repetition whereby you repeat the sexual command that has just been given to you

- Incestuous behaviour (this may not be full sexual intercourse but may be kissing an adult family member on the lips or hugging them for an unusually long time)

- Sexually disparaging comments about breast size, penis size, sexual performance

- Forced flattery whereby everything we do within the sexual union must be praised and confirmed as the right thing to do

- Positioning you

- Spanking and caning

- Sex with strangers (you and/or us)

- Taking pictures of you and/or filming you during sex acts

- Body worship for example having to kiss our feet

- Using you as a furniture, for example a foot stool

- Wearing a sign of ownership, for example a collar

- Forced masturbation

- Broadcasting your sexual vulnerabilities

- Making you ask for permission to experience an orgasm

- Cuckolding

- Misusing contraceptives

Owing to your strong link between sex and love, using sex as a weapon to abuse you will result in significant damage to you.

Any of the above activities, and other, which are undertaken without your consent and against your will are black flags. We will sometimes be subtle in the application of our desire to carry these acts out. We may label it as being adventurous or we will triangulate you with someone else telling you that they would do these things without complaint, in order to make you do them. Other times the approach is not subtle at all. In either instance coercion to perform these sexual acts and/or our behaviours amount to significant black flags that you are being abused. This would not happen in a normal and healthy relationship and just because we use our charm and powers of persuasion to bring it about, just because your self-worth is eroded so you "go along with it to keep us quiet" does not make is any less abusive. Why do we do this?

- Fuel. By drawing negative reactions, often powerful ones, as a consequence of this abuse we gainful;
- Control. We assert our dominance over you by making you submit to do things you would rather not;
- We despise you during the devaluation and using sex as a weapon is a means of punishing you;
- Owing to the way you link sex and love (and we know you do this) we are able to strike at your core through this particular abusive manipulation. It also means that our Respite Hoovers are especially powerful when set against this backdrop – when we make love to you tenderly again the effect and the relief that follows from you is immense.
- To reinforce our superiority;
- To condition you to do as we want. If we can achieve this in the arena of intimacy it becomes easier to enforce this control in other areas of life;
- To create situations and material to hold over you post discard, which will assist with the inevitable hoovers.

This is an especially powerful black flag and can often be missed because it is wrapped up in the pretence of doing certain things in the name of love.

9. Public Face/Private Face

We maintain a façade with the world at large. We like to show the world that we are a kind, honest, decent, successful and loving person with the trappings of success and most of all a loving partner and wonderful family. All is rosy in the garden. We are a great example of the way to conduct oneself in public and we work hard to maintain this façade. Behind closed doors we are entirely different to those nearest to us. Nasty, shallow and abusive. As soon as the front door closes then the mask comes off and the monster is unleashed. Nobody outside of the home knows about this and your protestations that we are awful monsters will fall on deaf ears because of the façade that we have created. If your partner shows one face to the world at large and a different, abusive one in private, then you have been ensnared by one of our kind and this is a form of abuse towards you.

I've always been a people person. They make me tick. I find it important to maintain that front of dependability and wisdom so that people know that they can turn to me. I carry out several roles in public life. I am a school governor, a non-executive member of a hospital trust, a trustee for a charity involved in helping the homeless and a committed Rotarian. I draw tremendous satisfaction from undertaking these roles. Happily, for me, my useful contributions to the various boards and organisations also means that I receive delicious fuel from those I work alongside and also the grateful beneficiaries of my largesse. I know a couple of people think that I am quick to cut-down unproductive suggestions and destroy pointless ideas but we are all giving our time voluntarily and rambling meetings serve no purpose, other than to irritate me. I need to drive the ideas forward and foolish comments are contrary to achieving that. I don't get involved amongst the foot soldiers though. No, I am never going to be doling out soup and bread at the street kitchen or leafleting on a cold night, that is for others. I am far better suited to the bigger picture, the grand design and orchestrating campaigns. I am a leader. This public face also enables me to ensure that should any of my crazy victims ever try to make trouble they will face an uphill struggle. I have at least one lieutenant in each of the bodies I detailed above. Their unswerving loyalty prevents any attack on my standing with the organisations I belong to. Moreover, such a generous and committed individual to service such as me could never carry out some of the defamatory allegations these deranged individuals come out with. Of course, presenting such a charitable face to the outside world is very tiring and that mask becomes so heavy so I am substantially relieved to remove it once the front door has been closed. Unfortunately for you, this means you are left in private with what lurks beneath. Try and tell anyone about what I do to you and you will not be believed. A behemoth of the community such as me cannot be touched. You would do well to keep that in mind and do as I say to avoid me having to unleash my rage.

This is a form of abuse for the following reasons: -

- The treatment you are subjected to behind closed doors (name-calling, physical violence, financial hardship, silent treatment and all the scores of other abusive manipulations) are clearly abusive in themselves;
- This method makes you feel trapped in a place where you ought to feel safe. Home is meant to be a sanctuary.
- You are denied the opportunity to seek help because we have brainwashed other people to believe us and not you;
- By singling you out for this treatment it will eventually cause you to think that you deserve it and that there is something wrong with you.

Why do we behave in this manner? Just like the manner of this particular black flag, it is a two-piece answer.

- We regard ourselves as the way we portray ourselves to the outside world. We want people to think of us in this way and we consider this to be what we are.
- The creation of the façade is extremely important to us. It becomes the device from which we draw fuel from all those who admire us for our supposedly "good" characteristics. It also provides us with a backdrop against which we can confuse you and make you out to be a trouble maker when you later try and pierce this façade.
- We want to be adored and admired by other people. We want them to herald our successes and see us as a pillar of the community. This provides us with fuel.
- We wish to punish you for failing us.
- We need the negative fuel you supply and adopting this two-faced persona is another device for extracting this fuel from you;
- It allows the emotions that are the real us, such as hatred, viciousness, envy and jealousy to be exercised and given freedom without damaging our carefully cultivated exterior face. In a way it enables us to let off some steam without fear of detection and the consequences that arise from it. Maintaining the façade takes some effort and in private we can drop the façade.
- We are still able to exhibit our power by treating you in this manner.
- It allows us to exert control over you as we invite you to "go on, tell everyone what I am really like, nobody will believe you. They think you are mad and ungrateful. Everyone loves me."

If you find that a family member, friend or colleague and especially an intimate partner behaves completely differently with you when it is just you and them alone then you are experiencing another warning sign. It is nothing to do with you. You do no cause or invite this behaviour (despite what we say and insinuate) it is entirely down to us as another form of abuse that we apply against you to achieve our aims.

10. Vacillation

If you find that a person switches, with no warning or understandable reason between being pleasant with you one moment and then horrible the next, then you are dealing with one of our kind and you are being subjected to our vacillation. We are often referred to as having Dr Jekyll and My Hyde personalities such is the sudden and remarkable change we undergo in personality and behaviour. Vacillation may not happen for many months. Everything is well and the golden period continues and then in an instant it is gone and you are being treated horribly. It happens in the blink of an eye and you cannot work out why. You will ask us what is wrong, what have you done and get no answers. We either do not realise we have done this (a lesser or mid-range narcissist) or we do and we will not tell you because that will undermine the power of this particular manipulative and abusive technique. Vacillation happens suddenly and with no warning. We will switch and then the horrible behaviour might last for weeks or it can switch back in a matter of minutes. It is common enough that we can blow hot, then cold, then hot and then cold again in the space of an hour. There is a repeated pushing and pulling which is particularly confusing, upsetting and bewildering. How does this vacillation appear?

- A friend will invite you regularly to come and have dinner every Wednesday evening and then will stop inviting you with no explanation given;
- Your partner always calls at 1pm to ask how your day is and stops this. When asked politely about it, you are told that they are too busy and can you not go a day without hearing from me?
- Your partner will enjoy lasagne one week and then hate it the next and maintain that he has always hated lasagne, until he asks for it the following

week and he will then criticise you for not having made it as it is "his favourite."

- During the seduction, your partner stayed at your house and talked about how he always felt safe and comfortable there. He admired the house. Now the shower is too small, it is out of the way and there is no full length mirror.

- Your friend has talked repeatedly about how she is so looking forward to a forthcoming concert and then two days before declares she does not want to and does not pay you for the ticket you bought for her.

- Your telephone calls were always answered by us enthusiastically, now we sound as if you are bothering us each time you call.

Vacillation will often be allied with some other form of abusive behaviour. A prime example is the silent treatment. Yesterday we talked with you (at you) for hours on the first day of our holiday. Today we are unresponsive and ignoring you. You cannot understand why but it is unsettling and upsetting. Why do we engage in this behaviour?

- We always see things in black and white. There is no grey to us. You are either with us or you are against us. You are friend or foe. Hero or zero. We cannot distinguish people on a spectrum but rather pigeonhole them into someone we adore or someone we hate and our treatment thereafter accords with that perspective. It is extremely disorientating for the victim because this splitting behaviour often occurs very quickly. It may be the difference between seeing us in the morning, going out for an hour and coming back and we blow cold on your return. Sometimes it is even a matter of one minute to the next.

- It is a defence mechanism. You have done something to offend us. It may be criticism in which case our fury has been ignited and we lash out, provide cold fury or withdraw. It may be that there is a diminution of disruption in the provision of fuel which causes us to regard you are plotting against us. It might be that you are dominating the conversation when we believe we should be so we will do this in order to wrest control back to us, especially in a situation where the ignition of our fury through heated fury would not be acceptable as it would damage the façade.

- It creates anxiety in the victim as you do not know which "us" is going to turn up. If it is "pleasant" us, then you are relieved and provide positive fuel accordingly. If it "nasty" us then you are nervous, upset and confused and provide the negative fuel. This change between good and bad wears you down and has you treading on eggshells. This then allows our other forms of manipulation to be applied against you.

- Naturally we gain fuel from your efforts to please us, mollycoddle us and then react when we are horrible to you.

- You compromise more often so we are able to as we please more often, in accordance with our sense of entitlement.

- We see nothing wrong in altering our position. We are entitled to do this. We must do it. Our position and behaviour alters in order to protect ourselves from your attacks and to gather the fuel that we need.

- The lesser and mid-range of our kind will not realise that they are switching. They will regard you as the problem. You are trying to belittle them and create a problem where there is none. Is it any wonder that they are cold with you or shout at you when you go on in this fashion?

- The greater of our kind understand how troubling this behaviour is. You are consistent in your dealings with people and you expect the same when people deal with you. You alter your position only with good reason. The fact that we change our stance and behaviour towards you and do so with no logical reason (in your world) means that this concerns you. It is one of the elements of our manipulative behaviour that you struggle to understand.

How is it that one moment we put you on a pedestal and the next we throw you from it? It makes no sense to you. That is intentional. By having you wondering and confused you will remain in situ and providing us with additional fuel.

Vacillation is common with our kind. People do not understand it. They remain locked into the relationship trying to work out why this happens and they will not get an answer. If someone behaves like this with you, you do not need to understand any longer why we do this, all you need to know is that this is a warning sign of abuse.

11.   Won't Answer the 'Phone

This is a form of silent treatment but most people do not realise this. Instead, somebody who is on the receiving end of this abusive behaviour spends their time focussing on the why and trying to resolve the issue as opposed to recognising it for what it is; a method of control and telling you we regard you as nothing. During the seduction period we would answer more or less immediately as we wanted to show you how attentive we are, how interested we are in you and then have the option of talking to you for hours to underline the connection that we have. We have already shown you what we can be like when it comes to answering the telephone. On the rare occasion we do not answer you know we will be calling you back in a few minutes.

During devaluation we know you are calling because we will always have caller display. If you withhold your number, we never answer those calls anyway and let our voicemail take them. When we do not answer the 'phone we are subjecting you to a mini silent treatment. You however will not recognise it as such because the way we have conditioned you to think means that you will find some other reasons. You will look for a legitimate explanation for this failure to answer rather than identify and acknowledge the real one. Accordingly, when you keep telephoning us at home, at work or on our mobile and there is no answer you tell yourself: -

"He usually answers promptly so he must be busy."

"He is probably asleep."

"There may be a fault on the line."

"His 'phone is on silent."

"He must be in a meeting."

"Has something happened to him? I must find out. I am worried now."

You will not think, at least not in the early stages, that I am deliberately ignoring you and failing to answer your call. I know this to be the case and therefore I know I can utilise this manifestation of the abusive mechanism that is the silent treatment on a repeated basis. Why do we do this?

- To draw fuel. Even though we do not see it we know that you will be thinking about us, possibly worrying and possibly becoming agitated. The knowledge that we are able to provoke this reaction in you through the administration of not answering the telephone makes us feel powerful.

- We are telling you that you are unimportant and beneath us;

- We may be preoccupied with another source of fuel. We do not want you interrupting and this makes the source we are with feel special since we are ignoring calls to concentrate on them;

- It keeps you interested in us because you are not getting an immediate response when you have been conditioned to expect it

- You begin to question yourself and will, through the salami-slicing effect of creating a sense of paranoia in you, end up trying harder to please us;

- It makes you anxious

- It is a form of control. We get in your head through this and stay there. You are unable to focus on anything else until you have spoken to us and ascertained that everything is okay.

- We are punishing you for some transgression that you have committed.

- We are able to advance lots of plausible explanations as to why we have not answered – I did not hear it, it was on silent, the ringer must not be working, I was asleep, I was out of the room – which causes you to accept the explanation. This lays the ground for us using this technique when we do not want to be disturbed, such as when we are committing adultery and if asked why we did not answer the phone we explain "I told you last week the ringer seems faulty" or "I was out of the room when you called," and this seems plausible and keeps you from uncovering what we are doing until such time as when we want to reveal it to you.

If your intimate partner or even a friend or family member regularly engages in not answering your calls when they used to do so promptly you know that there is a black flag flying.

12.   Talks About Someone Else

This is most often used in the context of an intimate relationship but can manifest in friendships, working relationships and the family dynamic. If you find that someone mentions somebody else a lot and they do so in a praiseworthy fashion, then this is a manifestation of the abusive technique of triangulation. There is a reason why this person keeps being mentioned. We will of course fuel your sense of paranoia by denying anything untoward if you mention that this person's name keeps cropping up.

"Does it? I hadn't noticed."

"Keeping tabs on me again are you? I wish you would stop thinking I behave like you do."

"Am I not allowed to have friends/other friends?"

"It was a coffee, a catch-up. You really do try to control everything I do don't you?"

"Well perhaps if you were more like them then I wouldn't feel the need to spend time with them would I?"

We will use mention of this person to undermine your confidence. Triangulation is often used in connection with other abusive behaviours such as disappearances, not answering the 'phone, flirtation and so on in order to fuel your anxiety. Triangulation comes in many forms and we often operate several triangles at once. You may find as our intimate partner that you will be triangulated with different people – someone we work with, a neighbour and/ or a friend. The advantage of triangulating by mentioning somebody a lot is that it does not actually provide any evidence of wrongdoing. You have not caught us embracing another women or found us lying in bed with someone else. We, of course, want you to react but it also provides us with plausible deniability also. Since when was it a crime to be friendly with someone? We mention them a lot because they are working on the same project as us/go to the gym at the same times as we do/walk their dog along the same towpath that we go for a walk and so on. What is behind this action?

- We gather two lots of fuel. One from the person we are triangulating you with and also from you;
- You will try harder to please us and allow us to do what we want in order to keep our favour when you perceive a threat to the relationship from this third party;
- It creates uncertainty, anxiety and nervousness which allows us to exert greater control over you;
- We are reinforcing the message that you are not special;
- We are suggesting we can attract other people, for instance we may claim we have no attraction for them but it is clear that this third party fancies us. That always stokes the fires of paranoia.
- It lays the ground for moving the "friendship" to another level (in the appropriate circumstances). We can tell you that we are having a drink with Joanne and there is nothing in it as we have told you numerous times before. Of course there will be something in it.

When somebody's name keeps cropping up, there is nothing innocent about it. It is being done in order to triangulate you with this third party and that is a warning sign.

13.   Becomes Someone Else

I mentioned vacillation above. This is linked to that but is actually concerned with the physical alteration which occurs with our kind. Peculiar as it may sound our physical characteristics seem to alter when we move into our abusive mode. I do not mean that our face becomes red with rage or twisted in malice, but there appears to be some kind of metamorphosis whereby our physical appearance alters. You may have noticed it happen but not taken much heed of what is behind this.

Our face contorts and seems to "blacken" our eyes darken, our brow furrows and our features take on such a distinct difference that you could swear you are now dealing with a different person. In fact, you are now dealing with what we truly like. The hatred, malice and venom which pours through us each and every day has an acidic effect on the way we look. It makes us appear vicious, frightening and aggressive. The other me, the one you usually see is a fabrication. A mask of agreeableness which has been fashioned from the careful scrutiny of other people and how those normal and healthy people interact with others in a socially acceptable and successful fashion. We spend a lot of time watching the way people behave and engage in extensive copying and mimicry. This is because we do not feel many of the emotions you do (because we have been created in a different fashion) and instead we have to replicate them. Many of those emotions are positive in nature – happiness, joy, warmth, caring and kindness to name a few – this means that we do not feel them and we do not instinctively portray a particular expression which correlates with that positive emotion. In **Red Flag** I explained how the Mask Carousel is how we choose an appropriate mask to adopt in certain situations. We know what response is acceptable and the one we should exhibit and we find that particular "mask" and then apply it. Accordingly, when you have seen us smiling, or showing a sympathetic expression or looking happy, you have been looking at the constructed masks. This is not what we really look like. When you see our features change this is because the relevant mask is not being applied any longer and you are seeing what we normally look like. It is then that you see the faces of hatred, jealousy, rage, envy, malice and vitriol.

Of course I can restore the mask in an instant and when you do notice that my features have changed you think that the real me is a creation. This is because you will not and do not want to accept that we really look so frightening. You will tell us that we have changed in the way we look and that you did not like it. We know full well what you are referring to but we will explain it away as only happening when we are upset before turning it round and pointing out that if you did not behave in a certain way, I would not become upset and therefore I would not have to look that. The restoration of the calm and pleasant mask feels much better to you and therefore you convince yourself that this is the reality because that is what you want.

Accordingly, if someone you are engaged with changes features to such a degree that they look like someone different you should take heed. This is a warning sign that you are engaged with someone of our kind.

14. Accuses You of Affairs

This is a common tactic that we deploy. It is a manifestation of projection which is one of our standard means of abusive manipulation. The accusations will be made on a frequent basis and we do not need to have any sound or credible basis for levelling the accusation at you. It will often come out of nowhere and appear as comments along the following lines: -

"You are wearing a different perfume. Who are you trying to impress?"

"I just rang you three times and you didn't answer (we never called). What have you been up to?"

"You are late. Been somewhere you shouldn't have?"

"Who was that man you were seen talking with in Jim's Bar?" (You weren't talking to any man there)

"You don't normally dress up like that (actually you do) when you are going out with your friends. You are meeting a woman aren't you?"

"I can smell sex on you (it is more likely the smell of fried food)."

"I found a pair of ear-rings in your car, don't deny it. Who do they belong to and what have you been up to?"

These accusations will be levelled at you with total conviction as if what we are saying is an indisputable fact. It is not the case at all but we want to put you on the back foot as we come out with these false allegations. We project all types of behaviour on to you but the accusation of you having an affair is a standard method of projection. Why do we do this?

- We are accusing you of doing the very thing that we are engaging in. We are having an affair and in order to avoid you detecting this we accuse you of doing this. This means that the spotlight of scrutiny is placed on you and not us. Some people think that this projection is a sign of guilty conscience. That is not correct. We do not have a conscience. We do not deal in our own guilt. It is purely a method of deflection in order to enable us to maintain control and keep you on the defensive

- We are bluffing just in case you may actually be up to no good so that you think we know and you confess. This becomes a useful way of getting information out of you and of course this will then allow us to go to town on your as our rage is ignited by your infidelity.

- We use the subject matter of an affair as the subject matter for this projection because it touches on a matter of love. You are a love devotee and any suggestion that you are being unfaithful will be morally repugnant to you. This means that our accusation offends you, upsets you and will draw a strong emotional reaction and accordingly provide us with fuel;

- The more you deny it the more we will believe that it is true. You are protesting too much;

- It provides us with ammunition to use in a character assassination or a smear campaign which are further forms of manipulative abuse as we tell everyone that you have been playing around;

- It allows us to exert control over you;

- You end up checking your own behaviours and minimising your contact with people in order to avoid the risk of being accused in this manner. Little by little, as we apply our salami-slicing techniques you will stop fraternising with certain people and even going out, because it is not worth the argument when you later come in to be accused of messing about with a member of the opposite sex;

- If you do go out, you are anxious in your return which makes you more susceptible to providing us with fuel. We may not accuse you of something and your relieved state will cause you to be more loving towards us;

- Our repeated accusations will cause you to try harder to prove you are faithful and not doing what you are accused of which means we are exerting more control over you;

- If we are caught out being unfaithful we will use your infidelity (fabricated as it is) as a basis for why we have done it and immediately blame-shift so our transgression becomes lost in the argument as you are forced to defend yourself again.

Projection is a key component of our manipulative arsenal. Accusing you of having an affair is something we will often do and therefore if you find that you are on the receiving end of such allegations you should be aware that there is a black flag up in the air.

15 Blame You for Everything

Nothing is ever our fault. Our superiority and entitlement means that we are never accountable for our actions or words. It is always someone else's fault and where you are the intimate partner of one of our kind you find yourself taking the blame for nearly everything. If you are accused of getting things wrong, blamed for mishaps, castigated for imaginary failures and lambasted for something not going our way (and this will be in the most minor way as well as major) then this is another form of abuse that is taking place. Your kind of course have your flaws but more so than most people you conduct yourselves in a manner which is decent, honest and according to a strong moral compass. You are considerate, obedient, follow rules and procedures, you do not break the law (okay perhaps the occasional speeding offence) and you treat people with consideration and respect. You are not a saint but you are not far away from such status and accordingly you are more likely to be blameless than many people. Not only are you less likely to commit blameworthy acts (unlike our kind) you also react with concern and astonishment if you find yourself accused of being to blame for something.

 One of my key defence mechanisms is the art of deflection. You may realise that nothing is ever my fault. It is evident why that is. I am special and above the regular humdrum vagaries of life that affect the little people. Accordingly, since I cannot be held to account, by reason of my elevated status in the world, it follows that nothing is my fault. I know this but I often utilise a method that ensures this state of affairs remains as it should be, with me blameless. I achieve this by accusing you of precisely what I have been doing. I am completely incapable of accepting I have done anything wrong because as I have explained, I am not subject to the usual rules and conventions that bind people like you. Thus if you challenge me for coming home in the middle of the morning, I will respond by listing the times you have arrived home late. I will accuse you of hypocrisy by suggesting I have returned late when you have done it several times. Usually you have not done that at all and this is where my tactics works so well. You are so flabbergasted that I have accused you of staying out late on repeated occasions, that you forget that you were challenging my behaviour. Instead, you switch to defending yourself by trying to prove that you did not stay out late on those occasions. I will then ramp up the antagonism by accusing you of suggesting that I must be lying. I feign indignation at this point and decide I will lose my temper. You cannot stand to be shouted out so you switch from defending yourself to placating me. Thus, your original complaint has been lost. I remember that your allegation was unfounded and invalid (so I can throw this back at you the next time you try and criticise me for something) and you feel bad for causing me to lose my temper. I have lost count of the number of times these conversations end with you saying, "I'm sorry, I was mistaken." I win again and this validates my belief that the rules do not apply to me (because you have accepted my position) and therefore I can do as I please.

Blaming you for everything is blame-shifting where we look to transfer our culpability on to you (or someone else) because of something that you have done or something you have caused. In your world there is no logical explanation for our blaming you but in our world it makes perfect sense. By blaming you we deflect any attack against us and also generate the means by which we can go on the offensive. Why do we blame you for everything?

- You are usually the most proximate person to us and therefore you are in the firing line. We will blame colleagues, friends, strangers, minions and family member should the need arise, so this ability to blame is not exclusive to intimate partners, but because of your closeness to us and your reaction you prove to be the most appropriate target;
- Blaming allows us to deflect attacks against us;

- Blaming creates a culture of fear and nervousness for you so you begin to anticipate that you will be blamed if something goes wrong – often it may be imaginary, for instance if we do not get invited to a dinner we will blame you because you did not spend long enough with the host at the last event. We will ignore the fact that this is most likely not the reason, because the invitees alternate through the year and in any event we did not allow you near the host as we wanted to speak to him. Once something goes wrong you anticipate you will be blamed, you are edgy, nervous and anxious;

- It asserts our belief in our superiority. You are the fall guy or girl and we are always unaccountable;

- We draw fuel from your reactions when you are blamed and you try and defend yourself.

If you find that you are repeatedly blamed for real mishaps and imaginary ones irrespective of whether you are actually at fault, or if you are blamed for the problems we encounter (real or imagined) this is another abusive warning which arises as a consequence of being with our kind.

16 Always Finds Fault

This is a cousin of always blaming you. With always blaming you, you cop the annoyance and derision from us in respect of something going wrong. When we always find fault it means no matter what you do it is not good enough. If you have done nine things out of ten brilliantly, we will completely ignore them and focus on the one thing you have not done as well. We will nit-pick and split hairs in order to find some kind of fault with what you have done.

I shall provide you with an example. I once went away for the weekend when I was living with my then girlfriend Elizabeth. There was a delivery of mine arriving at the house on the day that I was due to depart and therefore it was necessary for Elizabeth to take the day off from her work so she could take delivery. She did so willingly. I went away with my friends for the weekend and returned on the Sunday afternoon. Elizabeth had ensured the house was absolutely spotless from top to bottom. Everything had been cleaned, polished and dusted. Although we were not particularly untidy, it was evident that rather than spend the time on herself she had occupied herself with all those chores that need to be done but never quite get done such as filing away important post and documents, re-arranging the linen cupboard and so forth. The place looked like a show home. I could also smell the fantastic meal that she had prepared for my return. She showed me around the house pointing out the various things she had done. She did it in a pleasant manner, she was boasting but was merely explaining to me what she had done and wanted me to see. It was obviously a concerted effort on her part and done to please me. She also told me that her friend Vanessa had stayed at the house on Saturday night to keep her company. I did not like Vanessa because she did not like me. We were back in the kitchen after a tour of the impeccable house.

"So, did you have a good time away?" asked Elizabeth pleasantly.

"Why did you wash all the towels?"

"Sorry? What?"

"Why did you wash all the towels, "I asked again. My fury was ignited because to me, her efforts around the house told me that she could do all of that without me. She did not need me. She was self-sufficient and organised and independent and she was telling me she could do that and I could not.

"No reason, I was just in the groove with all the laundry so I thought I would do all the towels so they smelt fresh and felt soft."

"Really?" I asked with a suspicious glint in my eyes.

"What's the matter?"

"I just find it odd that you decided to wash all the towels when they did not need doing."

"Well most of them did and what does it matter?"

"Are you suggesting I cannot ask about the laundry arrangements in my own house?"

"God, no, it's just that I have done everything in terms of cleaning the house from top to bottom and the first thing that comes out of your mouth is asking me why I have washed all the towels."

"Oh I see, now I understand, you want to rub it in by showing you have done all this work to make me feel guilty for going away for the weekend."

"No. I am just pointing out that you have focused on one thing and missed out all the rest."

"Now you are telling me what I can and cannot say. I am sick of you trying to control me. You made enough fuss about me going away, that is why I was determined to do it."

"No I didn't," Elizabeth remarked as she looked astounded by my comment, "I had no problem with you going away, I even took time off work for your parcel to be delivered."

"Oh I wondered how long it would be before you brought that up."

"I am not bringing it up. What's the matter? Why are you finding fault needlessly?"

"Why did Vanessa stay overnight?"

"Why shouldn't she? We had a couple of bottles of wine and it was late so I said she could stay. There is plenty of room and she gave me a hand actually with some of the tidying and so on."

"Ah the plot thins. So you passed all of this off as your own work when you had help. It is starting to make sense now and you had Vanessa stay over, are you a lesbian or something?"

"Where on earth did that come from?" she replied.

"Fair question. I have to wonder why she was in this house to begin with let alone stay over."

"She is my friend," she replied indignantly.

On it went as I continued with my attack, challenging her and pointing out where one or two things had been put away in the wrong places, all nit picking and designed to find fault when there was none to be found. It had the desired effect on Elizabeth of keeping her in check and providing me with fuel. The fact she had done an excellent job on the house whilst I was away did not matter to me. I was jealous of her doing so and regarded it as her trying to get one over on me. Accordingly, I had to find some fault (admittedly there was very little to go on hence the comments about the towels) but I knew by deliberately choosing something ridiculous like that it would cause her to be bewildered, astonished and provide me with fuel. The comments concerning Vanessa were made in order to upset her even though I knew she was not a lesbian.

It I want to draw a reaction at work I will do the same by finding an apostrophe out of place in a report which is otherwise excellent and focusing on that much to the astonishment of the junior colleague. Why do we engage in this behaviour?

- As ever, it is a means of gaining fuel;
- It creates apprehension and worry which makes the victim more susceptible to trying harder and trying to achieve perfection, which wears them down all the more;
- It reinforces our superiority by enabling us to exert control over somebody over the slightest detail;
- It provides a means of belittling your achievements because we regard you as being in competition with us
- It allows us to decry anything you have done which is impressive and thus assert you are inferior to us

If you find that you are subjected to a lack of acknowledgement or praise when you have done something good or impressive and instead you are taken to task for the smallest thing (real or imaginary) you are being subjected to a further abusive technique at our hands.

17 Isolation

Isolation is another fundamental step that we take when dealing with our victims. It is present throughout the narcissistic cycle. During the seduction period we isolate you from other influences for two reasons. Firstly, to ensure that the more time you spend with us the more likely it is that you will be ensnared and the seduction will be successful. Secondly, to minimise the influence of other people who might be warning you about us, again to ensure that the seduction is successful. Once we have begun to devalue you, we maintain the isolation and again this is for a number of reasons. First of all, it is to ensure that you remain tied to us and providing us with the negative fuel. Secondly, it means that you are less likely to have support mechanisms which could minimise the effect of our devaluing manipulative behaviour. Thirdly, we want to avoid the risk of dissenting voices causing you to pull away from us. Once we discard we want to maintain your isolation. This is done by way of punishment and also to ensure that you remain vulnerable to the hoovers that will follow. Isolation accordingly plays a significant part of our campaign against you. In terms of its presentation as a black flag, how does it appear in the context of the devaluation? It is not so obvious as locking you in the house all day and banning visitors, ripping out any form of communication available to you and nailing the windows shut. The methodology of effecting isolation is often subtle and done in a stealthy way, through the tried and trusted salami-slicing approach. You should be aware of the following: -

- Making arrangements for you so that your diary is filled with events involving us so you are limited in options for you to do things on your own;
- Always answering the landline before you to screen calls;
- Asking who has called when you have taken a call on the mobile and quizzing you about the conversation so you feel uncomfortable;

- Standing over you when you are on the mobile 'phone and speaking to you so that the conversation is interrupted;
- Only allowing guests at the house when we are there
- Hanging around in the background if you happen to have guests so we listen in on the conversation and make you and your guests feel uncomfortable
- Always answering the front door to screen people calling at the house;
- Ensuring you remain by our side at events so we can speak for you and hear what you are talking about;
- Making it difficult for you to go out on your own (see above) so you give up doing so;
- Discouraging you from having interests and hobbies that do not involve us, we will do so by saying we want to spend more time with you, then using children and/or work as an excuse to blackmail you emotionally so that you stay in and we go out;
- Monitoring your online activities, acquiring your passwords (see below) either covertly or overtly in order to ascertain who you are engaging with and what is being communicated;
- Switching off the Wi-Fi or removing the modem when we are not in the house with you;
- Hiding possessions that belong to you so you cannot communicate with people or go to places e.g. car keys, house keys, mobile phone and purse;
- Smearing your friends to you so you bother less with them;
- Smearing you to your friends so they are less inclined to contact you;
- Preventing you from working by suggesting that you need to be there to look after the children, pets and/or the home or if you do work ensuring you spend little time with colleagues;
- Restricting your access to money;

- Removing modes of transport available to you, for instance selling your vehicle under the auspices of economising and forbidding you from using public transport as it is not safe;
- Driving a wedge between you and your family so attendance at family events is less likely to happen, either we are not invited or you prefer not to go;
- Making your interactions with other people difficult, embarrassing and unpleasant so that you decide it is too much like hard work and give up maintaining them

By isolating you using these methods and more we prevent people from showing you what is really happening to you so that you might try and escape us. By isolating you we cause the following: -

- Anxiety
- A fear of bothering with others as the less you socialise and interact the harder it becomes, it becomes a vicious cycle
- A reduction in your capacity to cope, accordingly allowing us to further out additional abuses
- Insomnia
- Depression
- Dependence on us

All of these effects mean you feel that you have no option but to hold on tighter to us and "hang in there" in the hope of a return to the golden period. Where any of the above actions take place they are designed to bring about a state of isolation which will prove extremely detrimental you and make it far harder for you to escape our clutches.

18 Jealous of Your Friends

We will aim to be introduced to your friends as soon as we possibly can during our seduction of you. This will enable us to identify those of your friends who we can charm so that they think well of us and will not pose a hindrance to our aims for you, to identify those we might recruit as Lieutenants from within your own ranks so they will carry out our machinations on our behalf and cause you all manner of difficulties and to identify those of your friends who are troublemakers and who need to be pushed to one side.

Normal and healthy people like their intimate partner to have friends. It enables them to have a life outside of the relationship and to bring something additional to the party in terms of experiences and activities. They will also enjoy interacting with those friends.

We however will exhibit jealousy in respect of your friends. This is applicable even with those friends that we have charmed and who like us. We will try and stop you doing things with them, we will suggest that you and I do something else or we will complain about you spending time with your friends. We will badger you to remove pictures from social media of nights out with your friends as we do not like to see reminders of you enjoying yourself with somebody other than us. We will of course deny that we are jealous and make excuses as to why you should not be spending time with your friends and why you should be spending time with us. It is a ridiculous situation because you love us and spend most of your time with us, invariably we will live together and therefore you would think that a small amount of time that you will spend with your friends would not cause such problems, but it will. Why are we so jealous?

- This suggests you have a life outside of us. We do not want that to be the case. We want you relying on us or everything, as part of our behaviour in isolating you as discussed above.

- You are giving your time and attention to other people and not us. This is denying us fuel.

- You are suggesting that other people are more interesting than us otherwise why would you be spending time with them if this was not the case? We cannot accept that you should be able to spend time with family, friends *and* us. We want to dominate your time because of our need for fuel. We do not want to share you.

- There is a risk that your friends may alert you to our machinations and thus interfere with our supply of fuel. We have no interest in your as a person per se, although of course we give the impression that we do, all we want from you is fuel and therefore if we perceive there is a risk to that supply we will react accordingly.

Any adverse behaviour that we exhibit concerning your friends such as stopping you seeing them, interfering in arrangements, calling them to you or vice versa is borne out of our jealousy. Stopping and interfering in your arrangements with your friends is a further abusive warning.

19 Name Calling

The use of insults, not using your name and adopting a nick name for you which you do not like are all examples of a further form of abusive behaviour. In a normal relationship insulting names are not used since the partners respect one another. They will use one another's names and may have pet names for one another which are private to the relationship and which are typically endearing. That is not something which we engage in. We use name calling or the absence of names in order to devalue you. Often the names will be used in a manner which creates doubt in your mind so that we can claim that the comments were made in jest, that we were joking with you and that you are being hypersensitive and that you are over-reacting. We aim to play down the viciousness of the comment after the damage has been done. Do not be taken in by such protestations. We use name-calling, horrible nicknames and deliberately not using your name as methods of abuse. As I have explained before we prefer to use words over actions as they are easier to wield. Insulting names fits that category perfectly.

Insulting Names

These will be used in a rage as we hurl them at you full of vitriol. We may whisper them in your ear when in the company of other people. We will base these insults on the vulnerabilities that we have found out about you. The aim is to unsettle you, upset you and label you. Your reaction will provide us with fuel. The range of insults will be wide but we do like to use those which insinuate that you are a lady of loose morals for instance 'slut','whore' and 'slattern' amongst others. You are a person of considerable moral fibre and to insult something that is central to you will hurt you considerably. The use of these labels is also symptomatic of two other things. The first is that it depersonalises you as a person with your own identity. This is because we regard you as an appliance which is there to do our bidding and by labelling you with an insult this reinforces this but is also representative of how we regard you. Secondly, these labels which use stereotypical insults of women demonstrates the misogyny which is endemic amongst male narcissists. For all our declarations that we love women (going by our track records we certainly seem to) the reality is that we hate women, despise them and this invariably stems from the relationship that we had with our mother or other female authority figures in childhood. By insulting you we are establishing our dominance and superiority over you whilst belittling you.

Not Using Your Name/Using the Wrong Name

Purposefully not using your name is again representative of how we view you as not a person but as an appliance. It causes particular upset and also allows us to draw fuel. Alternatively, we may use the wrong name when addressing you or a derivation of your name, for instance calling you Laura when you are called Laurel. This is done to underline that you are not important and we cannot even be bothered to get your name right. It is a simple but highly effective method of upsetting somebody. I would combine these techniques with a former girlfriend of mine.

There once was a girlfriend of mine called Lesley. My preferred method of gathering fuel from her and also manipulating her was to call her It. This was extremely demeaning and in line with my worldview that people are just objects and appliances to do things for me. You may be an admiring appliance, you may be an accommodating appliance and run around for me. Alternatively, you may be an enabling appliance providing me with what I want. A person is an appliance is an object. I was able to reinforce this especially with Lesley. I did not do it all the time. This would have diluted its effect. I would however be consistent in its application however. In some respects, it was a half-way house to the Silent Treatment as I was not acknowledging her completely, I was belittling her but not quite ignoring her totally. The fact I was talking about her made her feel as if she had to respond and thus I got what I was looking for; a reaction.

I would start first thing in the morning. As ever, I was awake first as I had had a refreshing night's sleep, the sleep of the just. She had probably lay awake for a few hours after I turned my back on her when she wanted to make love. She knew better than to pester me though. As I lay on my elbow looking at her freckled face, she would blink into wakefulness. Her blue eyes would meet mine and I would see the hope surge in them as she knew I was looking at her.

"Ah, it is awake," I would smile maintaining my gaze. The hope immediately became crushed and although she tried to hide it, I could see my blow had landed.

"Oh don't do that please, it is horrible," she would say pleasantly.

"It seems to have something to say. It always has," I would remark. She would shake her head.

"Please, stop it, you know I don't like it when you do that."

"It wants us to stop. It always wants its own way."

"No I don't."

"It is getting annoyed now. It is always losing its temper."

"Pack it in." She would rise from the bed and make for the shower. I would hover nearby and give a running commentary.

"It is washing itself using the shower gel we bought for it. It likes to smell nice."

"It is washing its hair now. It is trying to wash the guilt away. It reeks of it."

Lesley would try to ignore the comments but I knew from her sighs and the slumping of the shoulders it was getting to her. Having subjected her to maybe fifteen minutes of commenting on what she was doing, I shifted the tack and began to use this technique in a more suggestive fashion.

"It ought to wear a pencil skirt and blouse today. It does not want to look too sloppy even if it is a Friday."

Lesley would pick out the suggested outfit. I knew why she did it. She felt that by making this suggestion, even though I was still calling her it, it showed I was interested in her and she lapped it up. She completely missed that this was what I wanted her to do for me and was nothing to do with being interested in her.

"It really ought to cook breakfast as we must not go hungry."

"It would do well to ensure the shopping is done before we return this evening."

"It should remember we are going out tonight and it is not invited."

She would depart for work, bristling but not wanting to escalate matters. My technique would continue through the day. I would telephone her and ask,

"Is it busy?"

"Yes I am, so now you are talking to me are you?"

"It wants to know if we are talking to it. Now we are not." I would put the phone down.

By evening she would be pleading with me to stop it, tears welling in her eyes. Lesley had had enough of my objectification which was sustained and cutting throughout the day. As I picked up my wallet in readiness to heading out with my friends, without her, I would turn and say,

"I am going out now. I will see you later."

The smile that erupted across her face was immense as I had dropped the It commentary.

"Okay, have a good time," she would answer pleasantly.

"I will. Bye Karen."

I never looked over my shoulder but I knew how using the wrong name would hurt her.

Horrible/Embarrassing Nicknames

These are often used in public to humiliate you. We will call you by the nickname and invariably draw amusement and mirth from those assembled around us at your expense. It may seem silly or innocuous to those listening but we know that it hurts you for reasons which only you and I know. This will usually be based on something you admitted to me. For instance, I used to call a particular girlfriend 'glow worm' as a consequence of how when she was a child she would glow bright red with embarrassment as she was very shy. She found social functions intimidating and worried about them beforehand. Of course I was very supportive and told her I would stay by her side, look after her and introduce her to people. Of course when I did so I would refer to her as glow worm with the flush of red not far behind. This demeaned her and upset her, providing me with a double dose of fuel. One from her and another from the amused onlookers who thought it was just a term of endearment when it preyed on something which troubled her.

By using names or the absence thereof we are belittling you, attacking your identity, drawing fuel and exerting control over you through your identity. No matter how light we may make of it, how much other people regard it as amusing, this is a further black flag denoting abusive behaviour.

20 You Work We Don't

This is usually seen when you are involved with a Victim Narcissist. The Victim Narcissist is a low-functioning narcissist who wants to be mothered and looked after. For more detail on this type of narcissist and the other varieties you can read more in **Sitting Target.** The simple dynamic is that the narcissist is capable of working but will not do so and instead insists and demands that you do, notwithstanding your other commitments in respect of running a household, looking after children or other relatives and other demands on your time. You should be aware of the following: -

- The narcissist will have numerous excuses as to why he cannot work and you must have to. Often these will be linked to some kind of invisible illness that the narcissist suffers from. There are occasions where the narcissist has a legitimate complaint but even then it is not something which would prevent work.

- This is based on the narcissist's sense of entitlement. You are privileged to have him or her in your life and therefore you should do anything that he or she requires by way of thanks.

- He or she will think that he is above needing to work and that they should be a 'kept' person in accordance with their inflated sense of self. This encapsulates the logic (which appears strange to you). One would think that the narcissist would want to be able to show off his or success, demonstrate the superiority through how much he or she earns and exhibit his or her achievements and therefore work would be a suitable arena for doing so. The type of narcissist that engages in this form of abusive behaviour convinces him or herself that they ought not to work purely because they are so talented or gifted and that you should support them.

- Do not expect that because you are working that domestic chores (see above) and/or childcare will be taken care of by the narcissist. This is where the abusive element of this black flag looms. The narcissist expects you to support him or her but will not pull his or her weight in another way to provide something in the context of the relationship.

- The narcissist, by keeping you busy with work, home and/or children, is ensuring that your focus is on him or her nearly all the time and you do not have time for outside activities and more importantly that you are not susceptible to external influences (see isolation above).

- Keeping you busy in this way will maintained tiredness and exhaustion meaning that you are less able to deal with the other forms of abuse that the narcissist will apply against you.

- The narcissist will resist any and all attempts to have him of her work, providing a host of excuses as to why this cannot happen. Other manipulative techniques such as projection, blame-shifting, triangulation and denial will be used. If you point out that other people in other households that you know have two wage-earners or that the stay at home partner pulls their weight, you can expect responses such as: -

-

"Well he or she is an idiot for going out to work as well."

"I am not interested in what they do; they are not us."

"Why bring them up, we are talking about us?"

"So, you want me to be more like John do you? Fine, I will be like him. Do you know he beats his wife and has affairs, will that do you for starters?"

As ever these responses will seem entirely logical from our point of view (we are protecting ourselves, keeping control and drawing fuel from you) but make no sense when looked at from your perspective. Should you find yourself involved with somebody who does not work, shows no inclination to do so and will not pull his or weight in the home as a stay at home partner, then you will have been ensnared by one of our kind. You will, because this is the type of decent person that you are, make excuses for why this person does not work, no begrudge supporting that person because you love them and that is what people do when they love somebody and you are an understanding and compassionate person. You were selected for these traits in order for them to be exploited and abused in the full knowledge that you would be unlikely to complain about it. Another black flag has been unfurled although you have not noticed.

21 Fails to Message

The failure to message you during the devaluation period will stand in stark contrast to the blitz of messages that you received during the seduction period and thus makes the dearth of response all the more hurtful and bewildering. Ordinarily, we anybody else if you sent a message and you did not get an immediate response you would not be concerned. You would rationalise that this person is busy or away from their 'phone and besides the nature of your message is not one of urgency. You will, however, have been conditioned to think that we respond in an instant because you are so special and that we adore you. That has all changed. The speed of our response was designed to make you feel like you are the centre of our universe and draw you to us, whilst keeping any competition out of the picture. With the golden period over, we now look to devalue you and failing to respond to your messages is one of the ways this is done. You may give us the benefit of the doubt, again because that is your nature, but be under no illusion that the failure to respond to your message is done on purpose. Why is this done?

- To make you anxious and uncertain;
- To have you question yourself;
- To make you feel that we do not care about you;
- To increase your paranoia so you wonder what we are doing instead of messaging you;
- We may read the message (so you know this is the case) but still fail to respond;
- To provoke a reaction in you so that we draw fuel. We do not even have to see your reaction but know that you will be confused, nervous and possibly angry about our failure to respond to you and this will provide us with fuel.

This behaviour is designed purely to make your feel worried. If you raise these concerns with us we will of course push them to one side by pointing out that we were busy, that you cannot expect hear from us so quickly (despite us doing so for many months beforehand), that we did not realise you had messaged us, that the message was not important and/or that we were engaged in doing something else which was more important. We will be plausible in our denial and you will be left uncertain but accepting our explanation because you remain in denial. This tactic is very easy to implement because it consists of doing nothing but its effect is abusive all the same. If somebody used to respond to your messages promptly and now does not do so or fails to answer at all, do not be taken in by the excuses, you have witnessed another black flag.

22 Lateness

It is said that punctuality is the politeness of kings, but there is nothing royal or regal about the way that we behave when it comes to the question of punctuality. In common with much that we do, our punctuality and time keeping is impeccable when we are seducing you. We never arrive late. We appear when we say that we will (as well as appearing unexpectedly but that is a different discussion), we will be waiting for you when we organise to meet so that you are not left waiting on your own. We call you when we promise to do so and ensure that we behave in a punctual fashion. You admire this trait in us and it also underlines how we respect you and make you feel special by never keeping you waiting.

Like so many other elements of our behaviour this will change and signals that a form of abuse is being used against you and that your devaluation has begun. We routinely fail to call you when promised and then make up an excuse, which will seem plausible, for our failure. We will keep you waiting at a restaurant, outside a venue or even as you sit in the car outside a store or stand waiting for us in the hallway. By doing this we are demonstrating that we do not value your time or that we value you. Our time is all the more important and whatever we are doing, even if it is something mundane is considered of far greater importance than you. We will arrive home late from work, from the bar, from a sporting event and any attempt by you to point this out will be met with denial, deflection and then blame-shifting.

"For God's sake it is only ten minutes later than I said, can I not have a drink with my friends in peace?"

"I had a letter to finish. It was important or do you want me to make mistakes at work? Is that it?"

"I am not late at all. I never said that I would be in at 10pm. You are mistaken. Stop trying to control me."

"What's with the clock watching all of a sudden? It's a pity you don't apply that to your own life. You were late the last three times you have been out."

Three things are happening when we use a lack of punctuality as a form of abusing you: -

Firstly, we want you to become worried, upset and/or annoyed by our tardiness as this will have you thinking about us and your reaction will provide us with fuel.

Secondly, we are so absorbed in ourselves, we regard ourselves as massively important and you are not, that we will often actually forget that we are meant to be meeting you until you telephone us or message us asking where we are. If you try to upbraid us for being late, this will amount to a criticism with the predictable ignition of fury and you can expect us to react by shouting at you, turning up even later or not at all as we lash out at you.

Thirdly, it is often the case that we are engaged in gathering fuel from another source. It may be a competitor to your position as primary source by reason of our looking to prepare somebody else to replace you. We may be engaging in an affair to achieve that. It may just be that we are enjoying listening to a colleague praising our latest achievement, or piece of work and we are basking in the provision of this fuel so it causes us to be late in respect of doing something with you.

This lateness will not be the occasional and isolated event. It becomes habitual. We are entitled to do what we want, go where we want and see who we want. We are not obliged to be confined by timetables and certainly not ones that have been imposed by you. We regard any demands or instructions that we be in a certain place at a certain time as not applicable to us. We have no concept of accountability and we never apologise for our late arrival because in our mind we have done nothing wrong. Not only are we better than you and therefore not accountable to you, you should be pleased that we are actually gracing you with our presence and if we turn up half an hour late, then so be it. We also like to be late in order to create an entrance. This is especially true of events where we know people will be waiting on us and therefore we like to turn up late in order to cause a scene and ensure that the spotlight is on us, rather than the person whose birthday it is or on the about to be married couple.

Habitual lateness is all about gathering fuel from your reactions and telling you in an indirect manner that you do not matter and we are far more important than you and so is our time. Should you witness this happening with somebody you engage with and especially with someone who is an intimate partner you should be aware that this is a black flag.

23 Unresolved Discussions

Do you repeatedly find yourself thinking that you are never able to have a discussion with someone so that there is an outcome or a conclusion? Do you feel afterwards that you were never able to make the points you wanted to, that you were not really being listened to and that now you come to think about it, nothing actually was resolved? Do you make a point and then find that we respond by going off at a tangent, talking about something else or raising some different point which puts you on the defensive? Does the conversation never reach some form of finality or agreement? Is it the case that we talk over you, walk away from the conversation or just go round and round in circles? If you experience any of these, you are being subjected to the abusive treatment of unresolved discussions and this is a black flag.

When we engaged in ensuring that a discussion with us never reaches an outcome or a conclusion we are applying one or more of the following manipulative techniques against you: -

- Prevarication
- Procrastination
- Denial
- Deflection
- Blame-shifting
- Projection
- Circular Conversations
- Withdrawal
- Insults
- Talking over you

More than one of these techniques will invariably be used. The reason we engage in this before is as follows: -

- To frustrate and upset you so that you lose your temper, beg for an outcome or answer and accordingly so you provide us with fuel;
- To prevent you from gaining an admission from us that we have done something wrong. Remember, we are not accountable to you;
- To maintain control. If we have to admit you are correct or do something that you want us to do, then this means we have lost control. You (through your perspective) will not regard this as such, you will just see it as part and parcel of the flow of the relationship. To us we regard it entirely different and we see it as us ceding control, which makes us feel weak and offends our sense of superiority;
- It allows us to do what we want
- It wears you down. You would rather just let us do our thing than have to go through a laborious and circular argument which uses up your time and energy with no outcome.

When engaging in a conversation that will result in a lack of resolution, I repeat the same points over and over again. What I manage to do is sucker you into thinking that you might be able to change my position and so you keep going. Remember, as someone who is strong on empathy you have an overwhelming desire to try and 'fix' me, even though that is impossible. You really believe that eventually I will 'see the light' and understand the error of my ways. What you need to understand is that I know what I am doing, I understand what I am doing but I do not care that what I do hurts other people and especially you. The ends always justify the means with me. I have also created a false reality and therefore if you attempt to demonstrate something, which will interfere with this false reality I just will not accept it. I will claim that black is white and then the following day that it is orange. You cannot comprehend how I can maintain that position. It defies all logic. You know however that I am an intelligent person so how can it be that I cannot see this? You wonder whether perhaps you have not presented the situation in the clearest way. Maybe if you shout I might understand the point you are making? You are grounded in logic so you will keep going and going in order to try and make me see. The major difficulties you face are that firstly I want there to be a lack of resolution for the reasons advanced above and then secondly I have a different perspective on the world to you. My perspective makes my behaviour entirely logical to me but nonsensical to you so in any discussion you will keep trying to make me "see sense" and persuade me that I am incorrect. These conversations will go round and round and round. My behaviour will never change. More often than not the behaviour that you are challenging is not behaviour that should actually need to be raised with a healthy adult. You may find yourself asking questions such as these: -

"Why do you come in after 3am every Friday night?"

"Why wasn't this bill paid?"

"Why are you chatting with other women online?"

How do these unresolved conversations evolve? You will point something out and at first a reasoned discussion commences. This will go on for a short while and then you think that the issue has been resolved only for me to say something that shows it has not. My response will generally lack logic (to you) and be inflammatory. You then cannot accept this and you need to ensure I understand the point you are making so you repeat yourself. I make it feel as if the first conversation never happened as you make the same point and I counter them by not paying any attention to the legitimacy of what you are saying. This confuses and irritates you.

"Did you not just hear what I said?"

"Did any of what I said actually go into your head?"

"I've already told you about this."

I will recite the usual excuses, which often do not make any sense to you and round and round it goes until you give up or lose your temper. Not only are these conversations circular in nature they will also keep cropping up because there is never any conclusion to them. This becomes doubly infuriating for you. The conversation itself goes round and round. There may not be any resolution within the conversation but you at least think the point has been made and I won't do the same thing again. However, I will. The same behaviour is committed again and therefore it is as if the conversation never happened. You point out the error of my ways and off we go again. It is akin to the moon spinning on its own axis whilst going around the earth in the same orbit. There are two doses of circularity.

I am doing this because I know that you will give up before I do. You will become exhausted and stop making the point. This exhaustion then lessens your defences so I can follow up this abusive technique with an alternative method of manipulation. It also reinforces my superiority. I am right and that makes me feel powerful. If you were criticising something I had done, you have failed to persuade me that I was wrong and therefore I am validated to do it again. I am also trying to provoke you. Eventually your frustration with getting nowhere will spill over. You will start to shout or you will slam a door. You may storm off. This is all good fuel for me. It also confirms that my technique is effective so I will keep using it as I know it gets to you. I will also make a mental note (or I may even add it to my notebook) of your unacceptable behaviour so I can bring it up on another occasion.

"I'm not having this discussion with you again because last time you stormed off in a huff. There is no point in me trying to reason with you because you will only do the same again and I find that hurtful."

I am also doing this to deflect responsibility and also accountability as by now you know full well that these are two things I do not accept. I regard the unresolved discussion as a competition. One whereby my ultimate aim is to never accept the logic of what you are saying, where I never accept I am to blame and I want you tired and frustrated by the incessant going round and round. I demonstrate an amazing ability to keep talking and talking to maintain a position of not achieving anything. I will deflect, deny, reject and keep going around the houses, something, which will irritate the hell out of you when you have been subjected to some Silent Treatment as well. How can someone so talkative suddenly become utterly incommunicative? It is all about the manipulation you see.

Accordingly, if you feel like you are getting on a merry go round every time you try and discuss something with a particular person then they are abusing you by ensuring that the discussion never reaches a resolution.

24 Vices

Vices are a common with our kind. The reason we engage in various vices stems from several reasons which include: -

- Feeling entitled to do as we please;
- A lack of accountability to you (if it is for example sleeping with prostitutes which may be legal but morally abhorrent) or to the authorities (for example street drug use)
- The need to self-medicate to deal with any unease, restlessness, weakness etc. that arises when we may not have been able to gather as much fuel as is required;
- The circles we move in and the situations we become involved in may lend themselves to a greater exposure to certain vices (for example the Victim Narcissist often stays at home and therefore may spend much of his time watching television and eating), others of our kind may spend a lot of time in bars and clubs and therefore abuse alcohol.

We do not regard ourselves as being constrained by the usual social norms and believe that we can do as we please without repercussion or consequence. The greatest driver for our behaviour is our need for fuel which makes us feel powerful and omnipotent. Certain vices replicate that sensation (although they will not prove to be an equivalent) and as a consequence our need for our "hit" be it fuel or drinks, drugs, food, gambling, strippers and so on is great and this drives us to obtain fuel and also the sensation of power and excitement that comes from other vices. It is not the case that we will always indulge in such vices. Indeed, there are those of our kind who would not bother with them because they are able to obtain fuel readily and they also recognise that certain vices will hamper their prospects in that regard (for example excessive eating and drinking will affect the physical appearance of the Somatic Narcissist and therefore he is less likely to engage in such a vice). The presence of a vice however is an indicator that you are with one of our kind. The existence of a vice will also result in problems for you.

Strippers, prostitutes – infidelity, financial issues

Street drugs – financial issues, health issues, affects mood and temperament and behaviour towards you, affects ability to work

Drink – financial issues, health issues, affects mood temperament and behaviour, ability to work

Gambling – financial issues, affects mood, temperament and behaviour

Food – health issues

The existence of this vice in your relationship with one of our kind is not only an indicator but it will also result in problems for you arising out of our addiction to the relevant vice.

25 Reckless Job Behaviour

If a family member, friend or intimate partner exhibits an inability to stay in employment with one organisation for a sustained period of time, then this is an indicator that you are dealing with one of our kind. Many of our kind are extremely successful. We like to and have to be, the best at everything we do and the world of work is one of those arenas in which we like to shine. We want to reach the top, be the best writer, best performer, best artist, best provider of legal or accountancy services, be the best biller within the organisation, be the best sales person and so on. Our driven focus and the fact we are free from the hindering constraints of remorse, guilt and compassion allows us to tread on people and not worry about it in our quest to get to the top. We believe we are the best and this drives us on to achieve. There are those of our kind who are successful but they are not able to remain in the same job for long. They exhibit a reckless approach to their job. This arises because we regard ourselves as the best and will not suffer fools gladly in the working environment. We will not accept incompetence and because we do not feel empathy we are not willing to make allowances for people. Our treatment of people will often be haughty and contemptuous. We regard people as inferior to us, even those who may have seniority in the organisation. We believe we know best and that other people have it in for us. We do not respond well to criticism (see above) even if offered constructively and we will often find criticism where none exists. Our traits of superiority, grandiosity, boundary violation and a lack of empathy and our need for fuel will often result in the following behaviour in the workplace: -

- Arguing with colleagues
- Putting down junior members of staff
- Expecting other people to do our work for us

- Disobeying lawful orders from higher-up members of staff
- Fiddling expenses
- Stealing from the workplace
- Harassing other staff members and engaging in discriminatory behaviour
- Blaming other people for our mistakes
- Setting people against one another rather than getting the job done
- Refusing to work with certain people
- Engaging in the above behaviours with clients, customers and suppliers
- Telling other staff members what we think of them rather than being circumspect
- Engaging in office politics in order to further our own ambitions and gain fuel

All of this means that we are frequently complained about and generate problems and friction within the workplace. If this is brought to our attention we regard it as a criticism and our fury is ignited. With those of us who are higher-functioning we are able to keep the ignited fury in check and apply it in a way which does not cause us a problem concerning our job. We are also far more adept at using the above manipulative behaviours to advance our careers rather than hinder them. The lesser functioning of our kind however lack the awareness and control to keep their ignited fury in check. They will lash out and for example, will tell the boss what we really think of him which will result in disciplinary action and possibly dismissal. Alternatively, we will regard the job as beneath us and tell someone where they can stick their poxy job and walk out. We are however often able to get another job fairly quickly because: -

- We use our charm and seductive powers to "love bomb" a prospective employer to give us a job;
- We will tell lies about what happened previously to cover up our dismissal
- We will omit to tell the truth about what we have done in order to secure new employment;

- We are perfectly content to blame other people so that it is not our fault;
- We will pull favours to ensure we gain a new position
- We will sue former employers in order to bolster our negotiating position.

Accordingly, whilst we find it hard to hold on to jobs we are also able to acquire a new job with comparative ease. Thus, if you become aware that someone has a chequered career history and also if they explain it away as always being someone else's fault you have happened on an indicator that they are one of us.

26 Reckless Financial Behaviour

Similar to the way in which some of our kind are very successful in careers and others have a potted employment history, a diversity of behaviours is also evident with regard to money and a reckless approach to finances is a clear indicator that you have become involved with one of our kind. Whilst there are those of us who are solvent and use our financial resources sensibly, balancing largesse when required with judicious economy when appropriate, there are many of our kind who exhibit a haphazard approach to money and this is an indicator of which you should be aware. The behaviour will manifest as follows: -

- Never paying for anything even when jointly incurred. Expecting you or someone else to foot the bill for a meal of drinks
- Domestic theft. Using your resources for our use, such as always eating at your house but offering no payment towards the weekly shop. Staying often at your house (this is a red flag in itself) and then offering nothing to the pot in respect of bills.
- Repeatedly complaining about being broke
- Owing money to friends
- Asking to borrow money with no agreement about when it will be repaid (or agreeing to do so and then not complying with the arrangement)
- Taking out loans in your name
- Taking out credit cards in your name
- Stealing money from you
- Excessive spending when it is unnecessary
- Repeatedly referring to a pending bonus which never manifests
- Inflating our earning with no verifiable evidence to demonstrate true earnings
- Making reference to people "owing" us

- Failure to honour obligations such as maintenance and child support
- Spending on ourselves despite apparently having no money
- Incorrect priorities in terms of financial management, e.g. buying a new car because the neighbours have a new car when the roof needs repairing

There are a whole host of black flags which fly in terms of exhibiting reckless financial behaviour. Why does our kind engage in this reckless financial conduct?

- A sense of entitlement. We believe we are entitled to a standard of living. The world owes us a living.
- A lack of accountability. We should not have to pay for things because people should recognise our greatness and provide things to us for free. This is primarily applicable to the intimate partner. We are letting you in to our lives and therefore you should be grateful for that and in return you should support us and foot all the bills.
- Boundary violation. What is yours is ours. This means we see nothing wrong in taking your items to use for ourselves and especially so when it comes to money. This attitude manifests for example by drinking the last can of Coke in the fridge and not replacing them or knowing you have set aside some cakes for guests you expect and you tell us this, but we eat them anyway. This then becomes evident with regard to our behaviour concerning money. We treat your money (and that of other people) as belonging to us. We fiddle expenses, steal, use your money, drain joint accounts and incur liabilities which you will end up addressing.
- The need to impress people when we are in the seduction period. We lavish the target with gifts, holidays, fine dining and so forth. If we are wealthy enough to cover the bill, so be it, but often we will look to use someone else's money to fund our seduction of the new prospect.
- During devaluation we regard using your resources as a matter of compensation for your failure to provide us with the positive fuel which we require to such a degree. Using your money to fund the seduction of a new

target and our lifestyle generally is deemed as an appropriate punishment for your treacherous behaviour.

- Envy is a considerable driver in our behaviour concerning finances. We subscribe to the view that "we have one like that but ours is better". Just as we chase after somebody new and shinier than our present primary source we always have to have the latest, the biggest, the newest and the best and will do irrespective of our actual financial ability to be able to afford to do so. If a friend has a more impressive car than us, we will buy a better model even if our current car is only a year old.

How does this reckless financial behaviour become abusive?

- Stealing your money and/or spending your money recklessly
- Using joint assets as if they belong to us, which means selling them or charging them so your interest in them is depleted
- Failing to make maintenance and/or child support payments so that you are left in financial difficulty
- Unreasonable demands in respect of the financial element of a divorce
- Leaving you with large bills once we discard you. We are careful to ensure bills are in your name and not ours so we can just walk away from the financial carnage that we have caused.
- Taking out loans and mortgages that you are unaware of, in your name

As usual we will have plenty of explanation for the position we are in and we will do our best to persuade you to carry the can for our profligate behaviour. Any sign of a reckless approach to finances should be regarded as a clear warning sign that you will be affected by it sooner or later as another form of abusive behaviour.

27 Brings up the Past

We like to use the past against you. Sometimes it is something that has happened. More often it is something that has happened which we put a certain spin and complexion on and most of all we just invent the past. Remember, history is written by the victorious and we regard ourselves as always the victors. We of course never allow you to raise our past with us, it always has to be yours. This is one of the few occasions when we make it all about you and not all about us. It is an essential method of maintaining our control over you by bringing up the past. We are always able to recall some past wrong which you have committed or some particular transgression which we will use to suit our current purposes. Being able to bring up the past allows us to deflect your attacks against us, deny the validity of what you are saying and instead enables us to put you under scrutiny. We have a formidable capability for remembering what has happened before. It is as if each event in our lives together has been recorded in my mind's eye and in a moment I can locate the exact memory, circumstances and events in order to support my position and demolish yours. The pin point accuracy by which I can dredge something up which happened months or even years ago is quite staggering. It is all the more amazing because we always seem to forget about events which you try and rely on. Mind you, that is because you have such a tendency to make things up haven't you? It is quite a terrible habit that you have, lying in order to try and make me look bad or feel worse. It is not something you would find me doing. Absolutely not.

You abide by the concept of that once something has been put to bed that is the end of the matter. It is done. It is concluded. It is finished. We do not subscribe to that point of view. In fact, anything that has happened between us, which we need to resurrect in order to advance our case against you, is never concluded. It may be buried, but it is never buried dead. All the discussions, happenings and events, even though they may have been discussed, dissected and mulled over to an extraordinary degree many moons ago, are ready to be brought back to life in the click of a finger and thumb. That argument about the one time in the last six months when you actually went out with your friends (although that of course was not without a monumental battle beforehand) began when you returned five minutes later than when you said you would return. The discussion rumbled on late into the night until finally tired and fed-up you conceded defeat, apologised and sloped off to bed. All delight from your enjoyable evening having evaporated as a consequence of our ranting and raging. You knew it had been done to death. There was not really anything to argue about, not that that stopped us going round and round in circles in order to frustrate you. This argument was complete and there was no need for it to be mentioned again. Except there was. You organised to go and see a show with your friends. It had been in the diary for at least eight weeks and you headed away looking forward to enjoying it. It was one of your favourites, one you had loved since you were a little girl. You knew that we were not pleased, you could see it in the frozen smile you gave when we came out to say hello to your friends. Not of course that we were interested in being polite to your friends as they waited in the car. No, we wanted to see who was going. Checking up to see if your story was true. We kissed you and wished you a delightful evening although you knew underneath we would be raging that we had to make our own meal and we were left alone for the evening.

The show was magnificent and your friends excellent company but the traffic leaving the venue was heavy and you returned home half an hour later than you had estimated. Note it was an estimate, not a guaranteed time by which you would return, not that this fact would make any difference to us. You sent us a text message (you did not want the embarrassment of a horrible telephone call as you sat in your friend's car) advising of the delay and why it was. You received no response. That told you everything you needed to know. You entered the house and found us waiting, arms crossed and eyebrows raised.

"What time do you call this?" The accusation is launched. There is no hello, no asking how the show went or whether you enjoyed the evening.

"Sorry. The traffic was bad. Did you get my text?"

"Yes but that is not the point. You are late again. You do this on purpose don't you?"

"What do you mean again?" you respond, a knee-jerk reaction to the unfair accusation but as soon as the last word has left your mouth you know what is coming. You can almost hear the vault door being opened and the relevant deposit box being selected, the tiny key being inserted and turned.

"You were late the last time you went out."

"That was six months ago."

"It was five actually. It was March. It doesn't matter if it was yesterday or yesteryear, you are late and you said you would not be. You lied."

"I lied. Oh come on, you come in late every week. Either from the bar or some work meeting and I never complain."

"Yes you do. You complained last Friday and I told you that I had to meet those clients in the bar. It was a business meeting."

"You didn't tell me anything of the sort. I rang you six times to find out where you were."

"It was eight times actually and I did not answer because I was busy with the clients. As I told you. I remember distinctly explaining that to you."

"You didn't. You really didn't. Look, this is the first time I have been out in an age, I am home now, let me tell you about the show."

"No. You are not distracting me with tales about songs and dance routines. I am sick of your disrespecting me in this fashion. You always come back late when you are with those harpies."

"Why say that?" you ask hurt by the remark about your friends.

"Because they are a bad influence on you. They got you drunk that time. Do you remember? You threw up in the sink when you got in and then on the floor."

"No I didn't, that was you!"

"Don't try and twist things around. I remember distinctly seeing you stagger through the door because I was sat in that chair watching the news."

"You were asleep upstairs and I was not drunk. I don't get drunk."

"Oh really, I can remember at least five occasions when you have come how rat-arsed, banging into the walls and crawling up the stairs. There was that time you went with Sandra to that new bar, Apartment it was called."

"What are you going on about. No I didn't."

"Yes you did. Are you calling me a liar? Remember, I have a far better memory than you, yours is obviously addled by all the drinking that you do."

And on it goes. Past misdemeanours both real and imagined are brought up and levelled against you. Bringing up the past is good for all occasions. If you accuse us of flirting with someone, we will remind you of your brazen behaviour with our brother. If you complain because we have not taken the rubbish out, we will remind you how you forgot to pick up our drying cleaning on three separate occasions. Accuse us of over-spending and we will revisit your last three shopping trips and reel off every item that you purchased. The confidence with which we describe these past events has you bewildered and at times you are unable to recall whether we are actually correct or whether we are making it up. You often think that we are making things up but the conviction we demonstrate has you doubting your own recall. This technique is used by us frequently. It moves the subject of the argument on to you, frustrates, angers and upsets you so that you provide us with fuel and has you often apologising so that we know we have landed a blow and laid down a marker. Reminding you of the past, real or imagined is something we do frequently and is an indicator of abusive behaviour.

28 Controlling Your Appearance

We must always exert control over you. One of the ways we do this is by controlling what you wear. We tell you how your hair should look, what length it should be (forbidding you from having it cut is a popular method), how much make-up you should wear, what clothing you should put on and whether you should wear jewellery or not. You should be aware that our kind, in common with many abusers, like long hair because it gives us something to pull, just like a leash, because that is how we regard you; no different to an animal that is at our beck and call.

All elements of your appearance must be subject to our approval and veto. If we think you are dressing in a provocative manner, we will tell you that you look like trailer trash or that you look slutty. This will happen if you are going out with us. When you are on our arm at a function we do not want you looking demure but rather we want you looking like the trophy that we consider you to be. We want you to receive admiring glances (although of course you must not outshine us) and we can bask in the secondary fuel that comes with people then admiring us for having attracted someone as beautiful as you. We will stand and direct you in terms of what you should wear when we are preparing for a particularly public and special occasion.

We will undertake audits of your wardrobe and if we find items that are not to our liking we will remove them or damage them so you know that we do not approve. It does not matter if it is one of your favourite items of clothing or something that has been passed down through your family. If we do not like it, then it is removed. Our need to tell you how you should look is based on the fact that we regard you as an extension of us. Accordingly, how you look is how we want us to be regarded. We do not want you looking too attractive when we are not there as we do not want you receiving attention from potential competitors, but putting you down in terms of what you have chosen for a work's night out also allows us to spoil your evening before it has begun and remind you that you are answerable to us. Given that most of our victims are female in nature and although the balance is shifting, it is reasonable to state that woman take more pride and effort in their appearance than men. Accordingly, attacking and controlling something which is integral to your self-esteem is a particularly effective way of striking a blow against you, getting you to react (and thus provide us with fuel) and then cause you to submit to us.

During seduction it will be compliments about how fantastic you look, your sense of style will be praised and we will laud you for your fashion choices. We expect those compliments to be returned. Once devaluation begins we will commence our criticism of how you look and embark on our control. It will begin with subtle comments which may appear constructive on the surface but this is only to mask the true intent.

"That dress is really good but I think this blue one will suit you better."

"These trousers here will flatter your physique."

"I daresay you would look good whichever way you have your hair cut but I prefer it to be kept long."

"No you do not need much make-up, you are naturally attractive."

"I know I said the blue dress suited you better but that was last week. This outfit is much more you."

"Those trousers seemed a little tight to me, I think this skirt would be a better idea."

"You won't really suit short hair; long hair frames your face much better."

"It is a special occasion so you need to make sure you have full make-up on."

As usual we will exhibit our usually vacillation and hypocrisy as we prefer one thing one week and then decide against it the next. We will find plausible reasons so support these changes as we apply, once again, a salami-slicing approach to gaining control over your appearance. Little by little you will turn to us for approval, at first because you felt like we were taking an interest, then because you wanted to please us and then because you know what will happen if you do not do as you are told. Every evening we make you lay out the clothes you intend to wear the following day so we can approve them or not as the case may be. We will dictate where you should shop from, how much you can spend on clothing and your appearance. We will move on to criticising you openly when once we said nothing to complimented you.

"You have gained weight. Do you know how off-putting that is?"

"You have lost too much weight. It makes you look hard-faced and gaunt."

"Do you intend washing your hair this week or looking like a deep fat fryer all week?"

"Red really does not suit you."

The criticisms and rants that accompany any attempt of yours to assert yourself in the arena of your appearance will result in you eventually deciding, as it is the case with much of what we do, that it is just not worth the argument and you will back down and submit to our demands.

We want you reacting to our comments, first with thanks and praise and then later with upset as we pour scorn on your fashion choices. Your crestfallen silence provides us with plenty of fuel as we instruct you to wear a dowdy and neutral outfit which does nothing for you, when you are attending work. Attacking something which is central to your confidence and self-esteem also allows us to exert considerable control over you as we continue the devaluation. Any attempts to tell you how you should look (even if they appear complimentary in nature) are clear black flags that are being waved right under your nose. They are indicative of our desire to control you and have you doing what we want.

29 Control Your Social Life

This black flag is an amalgam of effecting isolation and control. It is a common form of manipulation that is often used against you by our kind. We will do it in a variety of ways, from making out that we have your best interests at heart to the less than subtle threats of what will happen if you go against our wishes. As I have written above, we make going out difficult for you but that is just one element of your social life and there is an array of actions we take which ultimately cause you difficulties in socialising. You should be aware of the following: -

- Arranging your diary for you
- Prioritising events that I attend on my own, forcing you to remain at home (to watch pets, to mind children, to economise or just because I say so)
- Agreeing to attend events that we can both go to without asking you if you would like to go. We always assume on your behalf that you are willing to do so because you are just an extension of us.
- Forbidding you from attending certain events
- Restricting your access to money to allow you to attend events
- Smearing your friends so that you are less inclined to want to spend time with them
- Remaining in the house when you have friends over so that we can "keep an eye" on what is going on
- Making it very difficult for you to have friendships with people of the opposite sex so you give up trying to do so
- Changing plans to frustrate your attempts at a social life
- Gatekeeping the telephone and front door to regulate who you interact with
- Demanding you tell us who attended an event, what happened and who said what to the extent that it feels like you are being interrogated;
- Turning up at an even unexpectedly again to "keep an eye on things"

- Stipulating times when you should return from an event
- Contacting you while you are out to again "keep an eye on things"
- Cancelling reservations
- Slating the places, you intend to go to, to cause to reconsider
- Hiding tickets and admission material to try and prevent you from attending

By controlling your social life, we are ensuring that you spend more time with us and therefore keep providing us with fuel. We make your social life a difficult matter for you so that if you protest and fight back you provide us with negative fuel. We undermine you so that you feel worthless and that your social needs are meaningless compared to ours. We are exerting control by preventing and/or dictating the terms on which you can socialise, where you go, with whom, how often and at what time. There will be a steady and systematic erosion of your freedom to socialise as we remove more and more of your independence so that you begin to decide that you are better served by not causing a scene and attending. Of course, once you start doing that we will shift our position again, all for the purpose of drawing fuel from you, by saying such things as: -

"You never go out anymore. Have you fallen out with your friends? That does not surprise me given the way that you go on."

"You have become really boring. You used to go out and now you just sit around at home looking miserable."

"You never give me any space do you? Always hanging around here. Why don't you go out or something?"

You will try to explain why you do not go out but try to do so without making it seem like you are blaming us because you know what will happen if you are deemed to be doing that. The effects of controlling you in this way means we gain fuel, isolate you and that has the consequent effects. Again we choose this as a method by which we attack and control you because you are the type of person who is well-liked (and thus we are jealous of that) and who regards socialising as an important part of your life. You like to interact with people, find out about them, talk to them and listen and understand and help them. We do not want you giving your attention to other people and we also want to strike at something that you like doing. We achieve this twice over. Firstly, by stopping you doing a particular thing that you like doing, such as ice skating or going out for lunch at a particular restaurant and then secondly because we damaged and disrupt the concept of socialising in itself.

Should you notice the steps being taken which are listed above, you are being subjected to a further form of abuse from our kind.

30 Hypocrisy

It is a common trait of ours that we exhibit breath-taking hypocrisy. We are very much of the mind-set that you must do as we say and not as we do. We do one thing and then contradict ourselves the very next day. We will accuse you of behaving in a certain way and express our disapproval of the same before going on to engage in the very same behaviour that we have complained about. When challenged about this we will deny and deflect from your accusation to such an extent that it really does beggar belief. You will struggle to understand how somebody can have so many faces, demonstrate repeated volte faces and think that we have done nothing wrong. We will tell you one thing and then do the other. We will hold ourselves out as being a paragon of virtue and then that very night we engage in all manner of vices. You are not allowed to challenge us concerning our behaviour. We expect you to accept it without complaint.

We do this because we have such a large sense of entitlement. We can do as we please and you are, because you are inferior to us, not in a position to rail against it. We are driven by our need for fuel. This means that we can adopt position 'A' in order to achieve fuel and then if we need to adopt position 'B', even if it is literally minutes later, we can do so without any hint of embarrassment or concern. The needs must. We are superior and entitled to do what is necessary in order to acquire fuel and you are not of sufficient standing to challenge us. Who do you think you are?

We adopt a hypocritical approach to much of what we do as otherwise we would not be able to sustain our quest for fuel. It also allows us to twist and wriggle to escape any accountability for our actions. All the while this creates bewilderment and confusion for you. This state of mind allows us to draw further fuel from you as you are hurt, upset and exasperated by our stance. It also plays directly to your need to understand and to make us understand. It is a repeated theme that our behaviour is such that you cannot comprehend how someone supposedly intelligent cannot see what they are doing is wrong and contradictory. We will easily and without any hint of embarrassment request a steak on Friday and then by Monday tell you that we hate steak and that we always have. You will be astounded and point out to us that we ate steak last Friday and declared how much we enjoyed it. We will deny that we have said that. You will sit open-mouthed at such a brash response and you will repeat that we ate steak the previous Friday. Surely we must remember? Surely we must know that we have just contradicted ourselves. Amongst the lesser members of our brethren there is no knowledge of contradiction because this is a knee-jerk reaction. Those of us who are higher functioning are aware of the hypocrisy but we are unaffected by it. We are content, indeed we must do this, in order to draw fuel from you and create a situation that because our denial is so firm, so concrete and so absolute that perhaps you are mistaken. Once this doubt begins to take hold we are able to then apply more of our manipulation against you, driving all manner of abusive behaviours through the gap created by your doubt.

Hypocrisy is necessary to draw fuel, keep you bewildered but most of all it is the starting point for creating an air of doubt in what you think and say which we can then begin to exploit to our needs. When you witness repeated and astonishing hypocrisy by someone you know and most of all an intimate partner you will have encountered another black flag of abusive behaviour.

31 Forget Anniversaries

The habitual failure to remember appropriate anniversaries and also to then not react in an apologetic manner when the failure is pointed out is a further indicator that you have become involved with one of our kind. I am not referring to those people who struggle to remember the exact date of their wife's birthday or the date of their wedding anniversary and have to have a gentle reminder, for which they are grateful. Nor do I include those people who provide a card and flowers one day late and who appear mystified that they have missed the date. Those people are purely forgetful and not of our kind.

The key determinants are as follows: -

Repeated failure to remember and adhere to anniversaries;

No remedial action taken when it is pointed our;

Absolute insistence on their birthday or special event being remembered, invariably including some obscure anniversaries (member of the golf club for ten years, fifteen years since graduation)

Annoyance when the failure is pointed out to them rather than an apology.

This happens because we are self-centred. We are only interested in the anniversaries which apply to us. If we happen to be married to you, we expect you to not only remember the date but the applicable gift that should be bought by reference to the number of years the anniversary commemorates. We however expect you to adhere to the anniversary but we do not have to. There is no excuse that we have forgotten, obviously because we have remembered in order to ensure that you provide us with gratification and gifts. It is a one-way street however. If we do provide something it will be done begrudgingly and we will mutter about there not being any need to make a fuss (even though we expect a fuss to be made towards us). We are not interested in you, only ourselves and by forgetting or pretending to forget we are reinforcing that we think very little of you and would much rather think about ourselves. It is also done to upset you so that you provide a reaction and accordingly give us fuel. Should you point out that we have forgotten, this will not be met with an apology. You have criticised us and therefore there will be the ignition of our fury. You can then expect us to walk out and disappear or for us to turn around and launch an attack at you with comments such as: -

"It's a fuss over nothing, it is only three years."

"Always have to make a scene don't you?"

"I hadn't forgotten I had something up my sleeve but I don't think I will bother now given the way you have been going on (this of course is a lie)"

"Why would I want to remember something which makes me so miserable?"

The occasion of an anniversary, whether it is birthday, christening, wedding, the number of years we have been together, your retirement from work or something similar will be kicked to one side and treated with disdain. You can expect this to happen every year because it is something to do with you and not something to do with us. It is another warning of our abusive behaviour by showing how little we think of you and how everything must revolve around us.

32 Spoil Birthdays and Family Occasions

This is the cousin of the failure to remember anniversaries but it is identified as meriting its own category since we go the extra mile in terms of causing a scene and spoiling the event. They happen every year and you have come to dread the appearance of both your own birthdays and mine. You would much rather neither have taken place if you are entirely honest. The day is spent treading on eggshells as you await the inevitable argument and dressing down that you will receive. The annual sense of disappointment will happen again and again and you hope somehow it will change, but it never does.

Let's begin with my birthday. You dedicate time and money to making my birthday an enjoyable and memorable occasion. I dedicate a degree of energy to ensure that it is memorable, but for the wrong reasons. You plan something special to mark the occasion and go to considerable lengths to organise a surprise party or a trip out somewhere you believe I will like. You scour catalogues and the Internet trying to find that gift you hope will make me break out in a smile. Most normal people will be happy with half the effort you put into pleasing me on my birthday. Not me. The occasion may involve a grand day out and a spectacular gift but just as it did last year and the year before that, it will end in an argument and us lashing out at you.

On the face of it, one would imagine that just for once we would get throughout the day without causing some kind of drama. After all, the day is all about us. Exactly what we like and what we want. People wish us happy birthday, they send us cards, they give us presents and you run around lifting and carrying for us (even more than usual). The spotlight is firmly on us. We drink up all this fuel but still we want more. Every single second has to be about us. Do not expect us to thank you or anyone else who provides us with a gift. Remember, we are entitled to receive them. We may have received gifts of twenty people but you know that all we will harp on about is the person we did not get a gift from whom we expected to. That becomes the focus of our irritation. The brilliant and thoughtful gifts are left to one side as we rail against this one person who has not bought us something. It does not matter that they send a card, it does not matter that we did not send them a gift on their birthday (and never have done), and it does not matter that nobody else would expect this distant relative to send such a gift. We will raise it and repeat it and rant about it.

Woe betides you if you do not give to us the exact gift we expected. If you fail to do this, we will comment and lash out at you. You cannot possibly love us since you did not give us the right gift. We conveniently ignore the fact that what you have brought us is still a wonderful gift and we actually do like it. That is not the point. It is not the gift we wanted and you will be subjected to our scathing remarks. If by sheer dint of exhaustive effort, you manage, against all the odds, to work out what we want (don't expect us to help you by explaining what we want, we expect you to know this through telepathy) and give us the right gift, do not expect smiles and thanks. We need to make a scene. Instead, we will remark,

"I see you finally got it right. It does not really make up for all the years you got it wrong does it?"

You can never win when it comes to providing us with gifts. We will always want to put you down no matter what you have done and irrespective of the effort and expense that you have gone to. We will always be unsatisfied and this will manifest in us giving you a dressing down in front of everyone at the party, or storming out of the venue at some sleight. Every year you will hear the same stinging accusation ringing in your ears,

"You've ruined my birthday. Again."

When it comes to your birthday the position is just as bad. We will routinely pretend to forget about it. Do not be fooled by our repeated apparent memory lapses. We have minds that remember everything and our powers of recall are spectacular. We know your birthday is on the horizon and with most things with us it generates two reactions. On the one hand we resent the forthcoming anniversary because it is a day geared towards the individual, namely you. It is not about us and we cannot stand that. It is rare that you ever allow the spotlight to be shone on you (by now you are so used to having to point it at us, you give up on it ever being fixed on you) but you do hold out the futile notion that it might still be done on your birthday, of all days. We find this galling. This is a day that will be about you and thus where will we get our fuel? Its approach generates dread and horror inside of us.

Conversely, we relish your birthday because we know, despite every previous disappointment, you still hold out hope that this year it might just be different. You pray to your own personal god that please, just for one, the day can pass without incident and you can enjoy yourself. You are not particularly bothered about doing anything special, perhaps a meal out somewhere and the gift need not be expensive, just so long as it exhibits that some kind of thought has gone into it. Your thoughts are based on hope as opposed to expectation. It will not be different because we need to spoil it; we need to make you feel upset and demeaned. To achieve this there are various things that we will do on your birthday.

1. We forget about it completely. If you mention at 6pm that evening that it is your birthday we will lash out at you by explaining how busy we have been at work or that there has been some other pressing matter which means

that it has slipped our minds. We deliberately forget about it and we will not countenance you criticising our omission.

2. We organise something lavish but we know it is not something you will actually like. As usual, you put a brave face on it and fix a rigid smile to your face. We know what you are really thinking because we know it is not something you like. In fact, it is more likely that we have organised something that we enjoy. We do this so that everyone else can see what a grand and delightful gesture we have made and we drink in his or her admiration. It also enables us to poke at you repeatedly suggesting that you don't like it. We are goading you into making a tiny admission that it is not quite what you expected and then we erupt in self-indignant fury as we castigate you for being ungrateful after all the effort we have gone to.

3. We buy some token gesture and point out that your 43rd birthday is not really something to celebrate is it? It is hardly a milestone. We then use this to remark on your advancing years and point out your various flaws.

4. We organise a lovely birthday for you but spoil it by turning the spotlight back onto ourselves. We turn up late, we flirt with a guest or we manufacture some drama so that everyone is looking at us and not you. We complain at waiters when there is a family meal out, when there is not actual need to do so. We want to make a scene and wrench the spotlight back over to us.

5. We remember your birthday and spend it doing what you want and we are pleasant to you until early evening when we deliberately pick a fight with you over absolutely nothing. The fuel we gain from this behaviour is all the sweeter as we have built you up, your guarded behaviour has melted away as we appear to have done everything that pleases you. We are waiting. We are waiting for you to feel good and happy and then we will cast you down so your emotional reaction is all the more heightened.

This behaviour is not just reserved for your birthday although we enjoy ruining your birthday the most. We do this with the birthdays of our children, friends and family. We hate it being about someone else and we hate seeing him or her being happy. In our world, nobody else is allowed a birthday and we believe that every day is our birthday and everyone should recognise that and act accordingly.

33 Physical Violence

Violence as a form of abuse in a relationship will come in many forms – sexual, emotional, financial and physical. All four are black flags and of these various forms of abuse it is the emotional abuse which appears in the most guises. Any form of physical violence is abusive in nature. There is never any excuse for it to be exacted on anybody but it is used regularly by our kind as a method of exerting control and extracting fuel. It should be noted that physical violence is more often (although not exclusively) the preserve of the lower functioning of our kind. This is down to two things. Firstly, the lesser functioning of our brethren lack the capacity and ingenuity to behave in subtle and complex manipulative ways. Physical violence is abrupt, effective and to the point. Secondly, those who are of a lesser nature have considerable difficulty in controlling their ignited fury. Those of us who are of a higher function also have our fury ignited and it is no less in intensity across all types of narcissist. We, however, are better able to control it and we have a greater awareness of how our ignited fury can impact on our image and the situation if it is unleashed against someone as heated fury. For example, we know that if we struck our partner at a function in front of people there would be significant repercussions. Our façade would be damaged and we would run the risk of losing sources of fuel who are aghast at our behaviour and turn their backs on us. Moreover, we run the risk of law enforcement being involved and with so many witnesses, our ability to charm and talk our way out of trouble becomes reduced. We are aware of these consequences because we are higher functioning and therefore we will control our ignited fury by withdrawing or doling out cold fury by way of silent treatment. The repercussions for you may well come later as well, behind closed doors. The lesser functioning of our kind would not be able to keep this ignited fury in check in this way and would lash out. Physical violence is a sudden and direct method of drawing fuel and exerting control. Whether it is a slap, a shove, hands around the throat, punching, kicking or the use of a weapon, those of our kind who are predisposed to using physical violence will apply a variety of techniques. I do not like to use physical violence because I regard it as something of a blunt instrument and beneath me. I prefer to use my mind instead. I also know that physical violence leaves evidence which can cause further problems by way of unwelcome questions and prosecutions. Plausible deniability is much bettered suited to other forms of abuse.

You will find that those who engage in physical violence will always look to smooth matters over once the fury has subsided. Meaningless and false apologies will be issued. Promises will be made not to do it again (which are always broken), there may be a restoration of the golden period for a short time by way of a Respite Hoover or a Preventative Hoover (See **Black Hole** for more) in order to try to gloss over what has happened. There may be promises to seek help and to change, but this is all talk which is easy for our kind to issue. This behaviour creates the usual dichotomy of you being a victim of physical abuse but then making excuses for the narcissist: -

"He loses his temper but he can be so kind and so loving."

"I fight back so I bring it on myself really. It just shows how passionate we are about one another."

"He cannot help it; he is just fiery but I know he loves me. He is always so sorry afterwards."

"He needs help and I want to help him. He doesn't mean it really, it just happens."

These excuses and more besides will often be made by you about our kind who engage in this type of behaviour. This is because you have been conditioned to behave like a victim, to consider whether you are at fault and whether there is anything you can do to help. These are natural empathic responses and they are why you were chosen in the first place by the narcissist, so you would respond in this way and not leave, or escalate the matter but try to help this troubled soul. The reality is there is no change that can be effected and the use of physical violence is a further manifestation of one of the methods of narcissistic abuse (although not just confined to narcissists) and is an additional warning sign.

34 Guard Phone

I have mentioned previously that advances in technology have allowed my kind to have a greater reach and to enable us to approach more targets, more often in a variety of different ways. This application of technology, through text messaging, e-mail, messenger, WhatsApp and various social media applications means that technology is a valuable tool in our desire to orchestrate our campaign to obtain fuel. We can have numerous prospects lined up, waiting in the wings to replace our primary source as we keep them dangling through our online flirtations. We are able to continue a malign campaign against somebody we have discarded. We can gather information on targets and keep our supplementary sources of fuel interested. We can use technology to carry out our triangulations. All of this technological weaponry must be controlled from a particular source and one of those methods of control is the mobile 'phone.

The mobile 'phone nowadays is a computer in our pockets. This device is the nerve centre of our operations and therefore it is where all our nefarious behaviour can be found and evidenced. The material that accumulates on our 'phones is extensive and demonstrates the devaluing behaviour that we engage in and also will hold evidence of infidelity and flirtations with other prospects. We assiduously remove this evidence after a period of time but there is often a risk that a message will appear on the front screen or there will be an incoming call with a caller id that we would rather you did not see. Often we will put a particular prospect who we are cultivating on the side under a different, seemingly innocuous name but we still do not want you knowing what we are doing. When we sit of an evening, glued to our 'phone, tapping and prodding as we send out our tendrils across the Wi-Fi networks you may notice that we tilt the screen away from you. If you try and sneak a peek at what we are doing, the 'phone will be moved away from you and placed face down. We do not want you to see what we are getting up to. You should be aware of the following behaviours: -

- Never leaving our 'phone lying around, even when it is charging
- Our phone often being in our pocket
- Using the phone so you cannot see the screen
- The 'phone left on silent
- The keypad sound is switched off
- Notifications are muted
- The 'phone occasional disappears (it is hidden somewhere in the house or in our car)
- Taking the phone to the bathroom (this serves a dual purpose – it stops you trying to look at it but also allows us a period of free reign away from your prying eyes behind the locked bathroom door. Of course we were just checking on the sport scores whilst using the bathroom. Stop being so suspicious about us.)
- Never answering the phone to you yet you rarely see us without it in our hand
- Irritation if the battery has run down
- Irritation is 4G is unavailable or there is no signal
- Taking a telephone call into another room
- Telling somebody quickly that we will call them later
- Evasiveness about who has called
- Being told the caller or messenger is but you do not recognise the name.
- Knowing that we have more than one mobile 'phone
- Secrecy concerning letting you see our monthly mobile 'phone bill

Our guarded behaviour is designed to keep our machinations secret but also to provoke a reaction in you whereby you become suspicious (although we will maintain that you have no reason to be like that) and you keep asking us who has been calling, what we are doing on the phone and why we are spending so long on it. All of this will upset, frustrate, irritate and anger you with the effect of drawing fuel from you. Our guarded 'phone behaviour will be masked by us declaring that it is our 'phone and nothing to do with you. Therefore, you need not look at it. This might be a fair comment in a healthy relationship where no guardedness is exhibited with regard to the use of the 'phone, but when seen against the backdrop of the behaviours which have been explained above, this explanation is merely an attempt to throw you off the scent. Our 'phone is central to our operations. We may not keep much evidence on it which if accessed could cause us problems, but if you are able to see the photographs that are sent to us, the messages and the calls as they happen then your suspicions will be confirmed. Our phone is an instrument by which we gather fuel from lots of other sources and also a method of drawing fuel from you. Our guarded behaviour is also a manifestation of triangulation. You are being triangulated with an inanimate object.

Where you see any of the behaviours demonstrated by your intimate partner concerning the use of a mobile 'phone then you should take note as this is a further warning of behaviour that is evidence of narcissistic abuse.

35 Porn

Porn is a staple ingredient for us during the devaluation stage. We may have encouraged you to watch porn with us during the seduction stage in order to 'get you in the mood' but also to engender a sense of it being a task that we do together. During devaluation we will no longer watch porn with you, thus taking away something that you enjoyed doing with us and instead we commandeer it as our solo pursuit. The availability of on-line porn is heaven sent for us. The sexual act with you or anyone else is the equivalent of masturbating using someone else's body parts. If you asked most normal people whether they prefer to masturbate or engage in sexual activity with another person, they would choose the latter. Ask us and we will say the former. This is because it uses less energy, allows us total control and moreover enables us to worship at the altar of self. Porn is the perfect vehicle for this. We will spend hours on-line looking through porn. Sometimes we may masturbate to it and other times we will not do so. By spending so much time watching other people engage in sexual acts we are reinforcing the fact that we would rather watch than do them with you. This belittles you. Furthermore, when we are watching porn we place ourselves inside the porn that we are watching. The sight of a buff and ripped man working his way through a succession of willing and vocal female participants is precisely how we regard our sexual performance. We are in effect watching ourselves perform and this pleases us. In the same way we regard our lives as a film with us as the star, watching porn has the same effect. We are in that movie showing all those women a fantastic time, exerting our sexual power over them. We will search through the internet to watch more and more bizarre pornography as we place ourselves inside each video in a position of dominance and power, or for the purposes of gaining ideas for our future interactions with you.

Alone in front a monitor or laptop we are able to sit as king in this sexual kingdom and become merged with the activities that we are watching. The knowledge we prefer this to you provides us with fuel, especially when you protest that we would rather sit all night in the study that go to bed with you. We will purposefully have a substantial pornography stash (downloaded movies, DVDs, magazines etc.) to boast to you about how extensive our appetite is for this material and also to humiliate you by showing our preference for this over you. Whilst we are able to control you during sex, both in the seduction and devaluation stages, we are in total and utter control when watching pornography and that appeals to our omnipotent and god-like sense.

The use of porn is also a place of retreat for us. As our interest in you has waned, we want to spend more time with the whores that we see on screen and porn facilitates this for us.

Our use of porn signals to you that we regard you as just an appliance in the sexual arena. We are triangulating you also when we engage in an extensive habit of watching porn. You are being triangulated with the people we watch and we prefer to watch them than go to bed with you. This is designed to make you feel worthless. Since you equate sex and love as things which go together, by suggesting that our sexual appetite can be fulfilled through watching porn, tells you that you are not loved and is especially hurtful. Being shunned for online activities in this way means that you are likely to react in an emotional fashion and as a consequence provide us with fuel.

We want you to recognise that we prefer to be alone with our imaginary subjects as we fantasise about them. We see these people as no different to you.

You are all actors in the film that is our life. We direct and choose with a click of the mouse as we would direct you once upon a time in the bedroom by making you adopt certain positions for us. You are all really inanimate objects which are there for our use and abuse. Porn is an especially hurtful way of putting you in your place, exerting control over your emotions and gaining fuel. If your intimate uses porn more than engaging in sexual congress with you, does so alone and extensively so, then you have identified a further black flag confirming you have become tangled with one of our kind.

36 Secretive Computer Usage

For the reasons outlined above with regard to our use of our mobile telephone, the computer, be it laptop, PC or tablet is also mission control for our nefarious activities. Our electronic tendrils radiate away from the computer, seeking out new prey and effecting a firm stranglehold on those already caught by us. The reasons for our secrecy in respect of our use of the computer are the same as those detailed above concerning mobile 'phones and do not need any such repetition here. Instead, I will focus on detailing the behaviours that you need to be aware of which indicate that our computer usage is for malign purposes: -

- Using the computer in a room which you cannot access
- Using the computer late at night
- Forbidding you from using the same computer
- Having two computers in the house, a general one for every one to use and one reserved for our use
- Removing the power lead when we are away from the house so the computer cannot be switched on
- Excessive use of pass words and pass codes on the computer
- The use of separate hard drives (these will be used to store pictures that are being sent to us and pornography)
- If the computer is in a communal area, tilting the screen away from you and/or closing down the screen if you pass nearby
- Use of the computer every day for more than a cursory check of e-mails for instance
- Exhibiting a preference to using the computer rather than spending time with you
- Expressing irritation if the computer is broken
- Expressing irritation if the power supply is interrupted, the device has run out of battery life or the Wi-Fi is not working/is slow

- Prioritising computer use over the children, attending to work, attending to household chores and social activities

Should you witness the above behaviours then you can rest assured that the computing device is being used for our machinations and that we are keen to triangulate you with the device and also keep you away from seeing what we are up to. It is another black flag of narcissistic abusive behaviour.

37 Read Your Post

In accordance with our entitlement to do what we want and do so whenever we want we do not respect your privacy. We have no concept of boundaries with regard to other people. This is why we intrude on conversations, invade people's personal space by standing too close to them and touch them, why we talk over people and believe that we are entitled to delve into other people's possessions and information. We have a general state of paranoia and as a consequence we must know what people are doing. We suspect people are plotting against us, notwithstanding our obvious popularity because ultimately they must become jealous of someone as successful as us. We consider that people will be looking to damage and disrupt our supplies of fuel and in order to remain one step ahead of people we must have advance notice and intelligence on what they are doing. This translates into us doing such thinks as opening your post, reading your e-mails and text messages and searching through your bags, draws and cupboards. We are not only entitled to do this but we must do this to maintain our state of omniscience. Accordingly, you should beware of behaviours such as: -

- Opening your post for you
- Reading you post once you have opened it
- Opening and reading your e-mails
- Opening parcels that have been delivered for you
- Checking through your hand bag and pockets to see what is in there
- Intruding on conversations that you having with other people
- Going through your cupboards and draws both when we live with you and when we do not
- Reading a diary that you may keep, both of the sort which is used for planning and also to record thoughts and feelings

This exhibits a lack of respect for your personal areas. We do not consider that you have them and nor do we believe that you are entitled to keep anything secret from us. Part of this is projection. We are plotting and scheming (though woe betide you if you attempt to examine our correspondence etc.) and as a consequence because we engage in this covert and devious behaviour we anticipate and believe that you are doing similar, hence our need to know.

It is also symptomatic of our need to control you. By knowing everything about you we can react and plan accordingly. We can also find reasons to launch an attack (for example you receive an invoice for something that you have ordered without our approval first). We use this, as ever, as a means by which to extract fuel from you by making you nervous (not because you are up to anything but rather because we will twist what we find and use it against you), by making you upset and angry. You are not allowed to keep any secrets. You are not allowed to keep things away from us as we must know anything and everything that is going on.

Of course you are not entitled to even ask us what is in the content of a letter that we may receive and any perceived attempt on your part to scrutinise our e-mails, correspondence and private areas of the house will be met with a predictable ignition of fury.

This behaviour whereby there is no respect shown for your privacy will be accompanied by paternalistic and condescending comments such as:

-

"I only have your best interests at heart."
"I thought it might be something important so I thought I had better open it."
"I couldn't see who it was addressed to and thought it was for me."

"I didn't think you would mind me opening it, after all you haven't got anything to hide have you?"

"You don't tell me things so I have to find them out for myself. If you weren't so secretive I wouldn't have to do this would I?"

"It is important that I know as well, you know, just in case anything was to happen to you."

Where you come across such intrusive and disrespectful behaviour you ought to recognise it at as a further black flag denoting our abusive behaviour of you.

38 Demand Passwords

This is an extension of our need to know what you are doing. Once again our sense of entitlement, lack of respect for your boundaries, sense of superiority, paranoia and feeling of omniscience drive this desire to access your computer and phone. It is entirely acceptable for us to prevent you from accessing our computers and insist on having access to yours, once again our hypocrisy is evident. This is also a method of control. By having you know that we can access your technological methods of communication, checking your call list, your messages sent and received, your e-mails and various folders, we keep you on guard. In all likelihood, because of the type of person that you are, someone who is honest and decent, you will have nothing to hide. This will however not stop us from seizing on anything that we find and twisting it to suit our agenda to attack you in some way. Furthermore, this will be used to make our intrusive behaviour appear legitimate.

"It is a good job I did get your password and checked your folders otherwise I would not have found this picture of you and this man, whoever he is. What's going on there then? Messing around behind my back are you?"

It does not matter that the picture is entirely innocent and was taken before we were together, we will seize on it and use it to our disadvantage. Once again there is projection. Since we know that we are getting up to no good on our own computers and mobile 'phones, we will judge you by similar standards and this will necessitate us combing through your devices in order to find something. We will apply various methods to gain access to your devices.

We will ask you to provide us with your passwords and pass codes on the basis of being caring. What if for example you fell unconscious and we needed to call one of your friends or a family member, how could we if are unable to access your contacts? We may need to attend to your finances if you happened to be hospitalised so it would be advisable to let us know what the password is and the other information that is required to gain access. Similarly, what if I need to use the computer when you are out and mine is not working, or I need to access an e-mail for you? I only need the password for emergency purposes, honest.

You may be amazed at how often people will freely provide this information to us. They are bedazzled and feel they can completely trust us and thus they hand this information over. If we meet with any resistance, we will talk about how it will bring us closer together and show just how much you really do love and trust us by letting us have this information. We usually get the passwords.

Should you refuse to do this then we will have to resort to alternative means to cause you to share this information with us. We are unlikely to be able to get every password from a different technique but what this does is provide us with greater leverage to cause you to share. We always start with your smart phone.

Obtaining your phone pass code is easy as we just watch what you tap into it when you are sat next to us. Alternatively, we will look at where the fingerprints are and then try the various combinations of where the marks are until it works. Our brilliant memory will store that information for when we use it. We will then use it to our advantage by not just having a look through your contacts, your emails and text messages that are stored on your 'phone. We will sift through your photographs and videos along with your calendar. It is highly likely that the number you use for your pass code for your phone will be the same for your tablet so we are in there as well. This trawl through your personal information is purely done because we have to know. It is what we do next that is the real purpose of having accessed your phone.

Best of all however is the fact that we will choose a moment when you are in the shower or asleep to access your phone and download software onto it so that we are then able to access your 'phone remotely. Having to sneak repeatedly to check through your 'phone is the mark of the amateur. We will download this software, which will then enable us to monitor everything you do. This will give us access to most, if not all of your information and thus we can keep an eye on what you are up to without you knowing. We will of course use the information gleaned to further our abuse of you.

Demanding to know your passwords and thereafter looking through your personal communications is abusive behaviour and a further warning sign that you are involved with one of our kind.

38 Provide No Support

We don't provide support. We are too concerned with ourselves and our daily hunt for the fuel that we need to be concerned about you. We are engrossed in our own world and have no interest in yours. The only time we pay attention to you is when you are providing us with fuel or you stop providing us with fuel. Everything we do is focussed around us. This is because we have to obtain fuel, as without we will disintegrate. The hunger for this fuel is never ending and accordingly all of our energy must be applied towards obtaining it. This leaves us with nothing left over for anyone else.

Being a caregiver yourself, you would like to think that the person who you share your life with, or who you work closely with, would be amenable to providing you with support. That may mean giving you emotional support when you are experiencing a difficult time or taking the strain allowing you to lessen the burden on yourself. You give and you are happy to do so, therefore why should they not do so as well? That is the outlook of someone normal operating by the norms and rules of your world. Those do not apply to us. We cannot provide you with support since we have nothing available to do so.

Added to that we do not know how to provide emotional support. Yes, we can see how chores can be done and the like. We also have observed the ways that you provide emotional support to other people and we know the phrases that are used, the expressions that are formed on people's faces and the gestures that are made. We have seen all that and we could trot all that out. In fact, we have done in the past. We did this when we were seducing you. When we wanted you to divulge about your weaknesses and vulnerabilities this will have invariably saddened you and upset you. It may even have caused an episode where you need emotional support. We were happy to go through the motions then because we were at the stage of investing in you in order to get our fuel. We were content to make the right noises, give you a hug and make the panacea that is the cup of tea. All of this was learned from others. We did not feel anything for you. We could not put ourselves in your shoes (heaven forbid that would ever happen) and we could not empathise with what you were experiencing and nor can we ever do that. Yet again, we conned you into thinking that we are a caring and selfless person. We demonstrated such an approach when we were first together and that attracted you to us. This raised expectation that you could rely on us and turn to us when the need arose. It is all false.

Furthermore, when you need support and expect it from us, you are showing to us how you are weak. We despise weakness. You will find that our kind is rarely found near children, the infirm and ill and the elderly. This is because they are all weak and want support regularly. We do not want to be reminded of that fact. We cannot be bothered with you cluttering up our route to fuel. An exhibition of weakness infuriates us. A normal person would see someone in a position of weakness and deign to help and assist. We have seen how this is a natural reaction in normal people. It will not happen with us.

If you are fortunate, we will absent ourselves from the situation in an instant. We will generate some urgent reason; find a pressing engagement we had forgotten about in order to ensure we can get away from you and your ailment, woe or injury. You probably will never see us move as quick when it comes to getting away from somebody who needs help. If we are unable to exit the situation, then we may just stand and look at you. You could be reaching out to us, eyes filled with tears of pain, asking for help and we will just give you a blank stare. We know we ought to be helping you, convention and observation has told us this, but we cannot do so. We are unable to leave but we are also unable to help you. This requires compassion and we do not have any. It requires us to us our energies to help you out and we are forbidden from doing so.

Our ultimate reaction where you need support from us is to go on the offensive. The uncomfortable feeling that you have generated inside of us makes us feel less powerful and smacks of inferiority. We know of only one way to banish such a sensation. We need to reassert our power and that means we must lash out at you. It becomes necessary to subject you to further insults and denigrating comments, at a time when you are feeling hurt and vulnerable.

"What are you crying for? I have had worse happen to me."

"I am sick and tired of you being pathetic. Deal with it."

"I bet (insert name of triangulated individual) would not make such a song and dance about it like you do."

"It's only a dog, you can get another one. Seriously, what a display over a dumb animal."

"You are hysterical; you need to get help."

"Stop crying or I will give you something to cry about."

"That's right; make it about you on my special day."

We will lash out at you with these words in order to make you feel worse and ourselves feel better because that is all we care about. We fooled you into thinking that we care about you. That is a fallacy. Do not expect us to support you.

Demonstrating our legendary hypocrisy, we will expect you to always be there for us. When we have a need you must attend to it straight away, even if you are experiencing difficulties yourself. When we have a scratch we expect you to make it better even though you might be bleeding to death before us. As with so much of our behaviour we do not regard the way we act towards you as meaning you should behave the same way towards us. If you chopped us in half, you would most likely find this stencilled through us like lettering on a stick of rock

"Do as I say, not do as I do."

This failure to provide you with support is not just selfishness, it is symptomatic of our mind set and also our need to denigrate you through never providing you with help and support, something which is anathema to an empathic person such as yourself. It is a black flag flying high and should be taken heed of.

39 Exhibits Cruelty to Third Parties

This is an indicator that is evident both during seduction and devaluation. During seduction we of course treat you like royalty. To our secondary sources we also maintain the seduction period for them for the purposes of maintaining the façade. In our dealing with tertiary sources (strangers, remote strangers and minions) we often are charming to them also but because they provide us with the lowest grade of fuel and because they provide us with an opportunity to triangulate them with you, the person we are seducing, in order to impress you, then we are often rude, cruel and haughty to these people. Such examples would include: -

- Telling someone to get out of the way
- Not saying please and thank you
- Shouting at someone who has misheard what we have said
- Berating a waiter for being slow or serving the wrong order
- Reminding someone in a service industry that they are beneath us
- Reminding someone in a public sector role that my taxes pay for their salary
- Reminding a public servant of their obligations
- Reminding someone the service industry that the customer is always right
- Making excessive demands on for example, hotel or catering staff
- Treating hired help around the home in a contemptuous fashion
- Not tipping people
- Demanding to be dealt with first and then complaining if we are not attended to immediately
- Over-reacting to a minor problem by demanding to see the management
- Inventing complaints to get people into trouble

Such behaviour is motivated by drawing fuel from the hapless individual we are berating but also to impress you during seduction and then to upset you (you feel sorry for the person we are berating or you are embarrassed by our excessive comments about the slowness of the service) during devaluation. We once again exhibit our huge sense of entitlement, our belief that we are always right and a lack of empathy as we have no consideration for the feelings of the recipient of our bile nor you or anyone else who is having to witness it.

We are also telegraphing to you that if you do not shape up and obey us when we expect to be looked after, then you can expect similar treatment. Behaving in this manner towards people is a product of our arrogance and our belief in our superiority over those that we meet. It may appear that we are merely standing our ground in respect of a sub-standard service or even defending you in some way, but it is the manner in which we do this. Rather than be polite and assertive, we will be loud, demeaning and hectoring. Seeing us behave in this way is a further indicator and also a warning that eventually you will be receiving this behaviour too.

40 Flirtation

We use flirtation repeatedly. We flirted with you when we seduced you and then we will use flirtation as a method of upsetting you when we commence our devaluation of you. We will always play down what we are doing by explaining such things as: -

"Oh her? Oh,I have known Mary for years, she is an old friend you have nothing to worry about there. She adores me, obviously, but it is purely one way, believe me."

"All I was doing was talking to her, stop trying to accuse me of doing what you do."

"You are over-reacting. All I did was peck her on the cheek."

"Can I not be friendly with people that I meet? Why do you always have to control me in this way?"

"That wasn't flirting, believe me, you would know it if I was flirting with somebody."

We are allowed to flirt. You are not. Such a contradiction should come as no surprise to you by now. We use flirtation to draw our victims into our web and thereafter as a mild form of triangulation to provoke an emotional reaction from those we are meant to be to commit to. It is entirely permissible for us to be flirtatious, although I do not actually regard it as such conduct. I see it as being friendly, taking an interest in people and fulfilling my role as someone that people are naturally drawn to. As I have had to tell jealous partners in the past, I cannot help being popular and if you want to be remain with me, you will need to get used to it. Naturally, I know what I am doing with the choice words, carefully gauged tactile gestures and suggestive comments. I am gathering fuel from the individual who is now caught in the glare of my sizzling laser beams, pinned to the spot by my flattering comments and witty badinage. All the while we can sense you glowering nearby, not daring to say anything or do anything to interrupt our display and more importantly our feeding on this fuel, but you are sufficiently irritated to provide us with another fuel line.

Once more we are entitled to speak to who we want and in the manner we choose We are of course gathering fuel and during our devaluation of you we are looking to find a new prospect for the position of a primary source of fuel and flirting with people is one way of doing this.

I have seen some of you decide that the best way to deal with us is to use our own behaviour against us. Admittedly, that can work with some of our manipulative ways. It usually results in us shutting off that particular technique and opening up a different front. Do not make the mistake of flirting in front of us however. You are giving us the green light to go on the attack. Should you do this, you have cut off a supply of fuel to us. You are not reacting to our treatment of you, as we desire, by you becoming jealous and silently raging in a corner. Instead you are being assertive and you are challenging our superiority. This is not permitted. Furthermore, you are making us look foolish in front of other people. Worst of all, you are telling the recipient of your flirtation that you are a free agent. You are not. You belong to us. You are our property. You are our appliance. You do not work for anyone other than us. You are telling us that we are not good enough and that you have found somebody better than us. We cannot comprehend that being the case. Nobody is better than us. Have you forgotten all the wonderful things that we did for you when we were seducing you? Have you cast to one side all the magnificent gestures and words that we used? How dare you throw all of that back in our faces? You are selfish, slutty and you disgust us.

This attack against us is on several fronts.

1. The removal of fuel;
2. The challenge to our superiority;
3. You are diminishing our standing.

None of this can be deemed as acceptable. You should have grasped that we regularly adopt double standards. What we do is fine but you must not do it and we will stand and berate you about your conduct having behaved exactly the same way only moments earlier and not bat an eyelid at our outrageous hypocrisy. We do not like it when people use our tools against us. We fashioned those tools, you did not.

If you are fortunate, we will log your transgression and then subject you to retribution once we are home. It is likely we will take steps to record your behaviour. You may notice this but emboldened by your assertive behaviour and also we can see you are enjoying the reaction you are getting from us you continue with the behaviour and increase it. We will make a note of what you are doing in accurate detail in our minds and ally it with some footage. Notwithstanding the times you have replayed our own conduct back to us, which we have denied and avoided, we will do the same to you. We will also make a great show of exhibiting it to other people to underline what a horrible person you are and your treatment of us is despicable. We will then exact our revenge against you behind closed doors and let you know just how mightily you have offended us.

In certain instances, the indignant fury that you unleash in us by flirting with somebody offends us to such a degree that we lose control there and then. We fly into a rage and haul you away from the object of your affections. Should they try and intervene they will also be subjected to our anger and more than likely physically. We will dress you down in front of everyone else and it is highly likely we will force you to leave early, our nasty insults echoing behind as we leave the venue. By this point we care little for what people might think about our outburst, we are comforted by the fact that we know it is your fault. Should anyone raise our explosion with us we will explain how it was your fault that we ended up doing this, that anybody else would have done the same in such a situation and invite them to speak to you, as you are the real villain of the piece, not us.

We will routinely accuse you of flirting with people even though you are just being friendly. You will find yourself, during devaluation, walking a tight rope of trying to be friendly (at our insistence) but avoiding being regarded as engaging in flirtation (because of the reaction that you will receive from us). This is intentional as it allows us to exert control over you and keep you in a state of uncertainty and anxiety. We may see things as black and white but we occupy the grey when it comes to much of our behaviour as this means you struggle to understand what we are doing and therefore you are unable to decide what to do for the best.

When you witness our extensive flirtation and also when you are accused of flirting when you are not, these are two black flags in the same category that are telling you that you are being abused and by a narcissist.

41 Question Your Sanity

This is a common tool that we deploy. We are always right because we know better because we are superior to you. This means that if you disagree with us, if you challenge us or do something that we do not like, then there must be something wrong with you. This abusive behaviour is used in tandem with the technique of gas lighting whereby situations are engineered to cause you to doubt your own belief and perception. A brief example of this would be hiding your car keys and when you are looking for them placing them back where you usually put them. When you declare that you looked in this place and you the keys were not there, we will tell you that you could not have done so otherwise you would have seen them. You maintain you checked the usual place but our insistence that you could not have done so otherwise you would have seen them, coupled with the fact that you will not think that we are playing games with you, will cause a seed of doubt to be planted in your mind. We seize on this and continue to gas light you. As fatigue from the other forms of manipulation sets in, you struggle to evaluate in a critical fashion what is happening and you start to doubt yourself and accept what we are telling you. You wonder quietly if you are actually going mad.

We cause you to question your sanity and we will also question it for you, by challenging you about your thinking and recollection. This is designed to upset you so that you provide fuel, it is designed to destabilise you and make you feel anxious, so you become easier to control and is part of the steady erosion of your coping ability. It is also part of us setting the stage for when we discard you. You should therefore note that if we question your sanity on a regular basis there is a good chance that you are about to be discarded. The reason for this is that we will also be in the midst of or about to commence, a smear campaign against you. Once of the main thrusts of this smear campaign will be that you are mad, you are mentally unstable and you are in effect losing your marbles. When we can point to instances where you have exhibited such behaviour (we conveniently leave out that we brought about this state of affairs) this reinforces what we have been saying about you and means that third parties are less likely to believe your (true) allegations that we have been abusing you. It allows us to paint you as someone who is unstable, histrionic and prone to making things up. With evidence of this from during the relationship, which as an honest person you will even admit to as well, this creates a toxic position for you. You have been led to believe through our manipulative behaviour that you have been forgetful, over-reacting and acting erratically. We will have engineered this so other people have seen it. You will be tired and worn down and this further manipulation will cause you to react. You will not be calm and reasoned, but on edge, frazzled and at your wits' end, which all plays into our hands.

The repeated questioning of your sanity will as ever allow us to draw fuel from you, it allows us to exert control because after a while you start to believe we are right and that you are "going mad" so you go along with what we suggest. Most of all it allows us to create a platform and background so that when we discard you, you are isolated from people who might help you and they will most likely not believe what you are saying about us.

No matter how concerned we may appear to be about your mental state, no matter how often we try to get you to see doctors (another way of building up a platform for the eventual declaration that you are unstable) this is not borne out of concern, it is a method of abuse and manipulation. You should also take note that this tactic is favoured by those of our kind who share children with you. It is a hammer blow to your attempts to gain residence of your children if your mental capacity is questioned. It also means that we "get in first" because we know that you will accuse us of being the abuser and a manipulator and this enables us to point out that again you are making things up because you are unstable and we point to previous instances where the doctor was called out to see you, or where an incident was logged with the police, in order to maintain the fiction that it is you who is unstable and a danger. You should be very wary of any attempts to paint you as unstable and any attempts to question your sanity. This is a particularly dangerous and insidious method of undermining you on several levels.

42 Put You Down in Front of Others

Most healthy people in normal relationships support one another. If they have a disagreement it is discussed in private and in a mature and reasonable manner in order to reach a resolution. There is a mutual respect which means that the parties to that relationship do not engage in denigrating behaviour towards one another and certainly not in front of other people. We engage in this behaviour as a means of demonstrating our innate superiority, drawing fuel and controlling you.

During seduction we sing your praises and delight in telling everybody how wonderful you are. Like so many other manipulative and abusive steps we are setting you up for a fall. Once we commence our devaluation of you, we will start to put your down in front of other people. This will upset and frustrate you so that you will provide us with negative fuel. Initially, those witnessing it will find it more amusing than nasty and their responses will provide us with positive fuel as they laugh at our comment. Over time this behaviour worsens so that you are made to feel stupid and awkward in front of people. You should be aware of the following:

-

- Talking over you;
- Eye-rolling
- Making snorts of derision
- Using an embarrassing nickname for you
- Adopting a patronising tone, "Yes darling, we all know that but the point being made was as follows…"
- Undermining your opinion
- Delighting in pointing out that you are wrong
- Cutting you off when you are trying to make a point
- Changing the subject when you are speaking
- Addressing somebody else when you are speaking

- Dropping something so that everyone is distracted such as spilling a drink or breaking a plate
- Pointing out something going on elsewhere when you are trying to talk
- Calling you an insulting name
- Glaring at you

These behaviours will either be an implicit put down, for example by talking over you so that we suggest what you have to say is of no importance or it will be a direct insult whereby we upbraid you in front of other people. This is all about drawing fuel and exerting control over you in a public setting. You are our appliance and we decide when and how you should operate. If you are amongst our coterie you will find nobody will ride to your defence and instead you will be left upset and quite possibly facing several people laughing at your discomfort. If the audience is neutral, then the put downs will be of a more implicit nature.

One of the main reasons we put you down in this manner is because you are taking the spotlight away from us and we do not like that. You are there to make us look good, to ensure that you support us and to facilitate the shining of the spotlight on us at all times. You should laugh at our jokes, smile at our anecdotes (even though you have heard them scores of times) and lead the applause when required. We regard you as competition to us and if you begin to shine in any way around us then we must clamp down on your swiftly and firmly. This is done by putting you down. One of my former girlfriends, Paula, was an excellent conversationalist and a real boon at dinner parties. This recollection is for her and serves as a particularly effective example of how this abusive technique is used.

You always dreaded going to a dinner party with me. In the golden period you could not get enough of them. You marvelled at how engaging my friends were, how welcome they made you feel and you delighted in the range and standard of cuisine. Your knowledge of wine is pretty extensive and people regularly sought out your opinion of the selection they had bought. They even began to call you beforehand to seek recommendations and of course you were always happy to help. I of course enjoyed parading you as my new acquisition amongst my friends and at formal dinners associated with work.

It did not take long however for your informative opinions about wine to begin to annoy me. How I hated that the spotlight lingered on you for so long as people asked you questions and listened attentively to your opinions. My attempts at talking about my accomplishments took a back-seat to you and your wine tasting show. I barely kept my rage in check. How dare you hog their attention in this manner, they were my friends, not yours. The fury boiled away beneath the surface as all faces turned towards you leaving me stranded at the head of the table. Of course, I could not let this behaviour go unchallenged. Initially, I suggested, after dinner in the taxi home that you might want to lessen the amount of time you spoke about one of your favourite topics.

"I know everyone seems to be paying you attention, " I would explain, "but they are just being polite. I did hear Christine comment that you seemed something of the know-it-all about wine. Perhaps you should tone it down for next time."

You look surprised (not least because Christine said quite the contrary but I knew you disliked confrontation and would not challenge her about her supposed remark) but eager to please you apologised and said you had not realised you had held the floor for such a long time.

After that I continued to chip away with my remarks before we attended a dinner party (even though you had not long been off the phone to the host who had called to ask for your advice) in order to diminish your confidence.

"But John just called me and sought my advice about the rioja," you declared.

"I know but that is purely to please me darling, he wants work from me and thinks he can curry favour by speaking to you and seeking your views."

"Oh" was all you can muster to my further lie.

I would caution you each time against hogging the limelight and remind you that other people had opinions they might like to share as well. I would theatrically cough when I regarded you as talking for too long and you would hastily end your appraisal of the Chablis.

The next dinner party when somebody poured the wine into your glass first and asked you to take the group through what you tasted, you glanced at me. I sat smiling but my glare was cold and unmistakable. You sipped the wine and declared,

"It is very good, very fruity," and said no more. You looked back to me and I gave you my nod of approval at how you were learning.

Once I had reduced your wine observations to the occasional sentence I would move on to actively putting you down with back-handed compliments and insinuated remarks. Few of those attending seemed to notice but I knew you did from the reddening of the skin on your chest and neck as embarrassment flushed across you. I would accuse you of flirting with other male guests even when you were just making your usual polite and charming conversation. Like slicing a salami, I cut away at you, eroding your confidence and demeaning you steadily and effectively until you began to feign illness to avoid attending dinner parties. Of course I would not let that happen as I wanted you, my beautiful girlfriend on my arm, since appearances had to be maintained and besides, how else might I continue my campaign of belittlement without being in the glare of that powerful spotlight?

Your recalcitrance increased until you would sit barely speaking which resulted in me giving you a dressing down once we reached home. That was a night you would not forget. After that I decided that you were of no more use to me at dinner parties, I could not have my brilliant anecdotes undermined by someone who never said much and rarely laughed. Kathryn was invited to the next dinner party instead.

If you experience such put-downs and controlling behaviour in a public environment, then you ought to be aware that this is further evidence of the abusive technique being applied against you.

43 Second Guessing

When we seduce you, it will often seem as if we can read your mind. We know all the things that you like and those that you do not like. We buy you things which you love, we take you to places that you enjoy and we appear to understand you like nobody else. This is all testament to the preparatory work we undertook when we decided to target you and our capacity for gathering information about you. You may be forgiven for thinking that we are able to second guess what you want. Since we behave as if we are able to do this, when we decide to devalue you, we decide that you should return the compliment and be able to anticipate our needs even though that is a thankless task given our inherently contradictory and volatile natures. We however expect this of you, firstly because we gave you similar and secondly because it affords us an excellent method of controlling you and abusing you. We want and demand that you spend your time trying to second-guess what we will say and do. This makes us feel powerful and omniscient and at the same time it will exhaust you and leave you unable to cope. This lessens the risk that you will find the strength to try to leave us and remove that supply which we hold so dear.

Through the application of our manipulative techniques we push you into a position where you are left having to ascertain what we might do in order to please us and most of all to try to escape our wrath. This is a near constant state of vigilance where you are treading on eggshells as you try to negotiate your way through another day. It is hard. It is unpredictable. It is designed to condition you to our way of thinking so that you keep on supplying us. It is a method of control and it is utterly damaging to you.

We enjoy you trying to second-guess what we do so much because it makes us feel like a god. Before you do anything you must consider whether it will please or annoy us. It also strips you of your identity. You no longer think for yourself but you have to change your thinking to consider what we want. I wrote above how you can never make us see the world in the way that you do. Not only will we not change so that can be achieved, we will alter the way you look at the world. We force you to regard the world through our eyes. Your decisions are no longer your own as everything must be considered against our matrix. You become our attachment, your self-esteem melts away and you become our appliance. We regard getting you to this position as the pinnacle of achievement. You have become an automaton that is geared to establishing what our needs are and fulfilling them. Should you not do so then you will suffer the consequences by being subjected to one of our vicious rages.

The problem you face is that we cannot be completely second-guessed because we keep changing the rules and the circumstances. I have written elsewhere how some people regard being ensnared by a narcissist as being trapped in some kind of prison. It is worse than that. In prison there are rules and conventions which if obeyed means that your period of incarceration will pass quicker and without incident. Stand in that place, be quiet at this time, and do not look at him. Rules both formal and informal to be adhered to so that you do not feel the wrath of prisoner or prisoner guard. There are no such rules when we trap you. It is akin to being in a concentration camp where as the camp commandant we can do as we please, whenever we please and in whatever manner suits us and you have no way of knowing whether the next thing that you will do will lead to you being shot. The way we change our minds and our behaviours, so that last week we liked a particular food but now we do not want to eat it makes your life extremely difficult. Not only is this random nature difficult to address, when you fail to do as required (and you will) you are punished with blistering fury at your failure to appreciate us and give us what we want. You are expected to know at all times what we will want and need, even if it changes at a moment's notice.

Someone who is subjected to his for long periods will be made ill. The hyper vigilance combined with the erratic behaviour and repeated chastisement will take its toll on you. Trying to second-guess us is exhausting and ultimately futile. Yes, we want it but the cost to you of doing this will be substantial. You lose your identity and your sense of self. You are exhausted and anxious from being a state of high alertness nearly all the time. You feel unsettled and jumpy. You forget who you are and the concept of relaxation has become alien to you. You are treated horrendously being insulted and shouted at when all you have tried to do is the right thing. Subjected to this for any length of time will result in a major breakdown for you. We love to have you second guessing us because it really does demonstrate to us that we have achieved considerable control over you. It makes us feel powerful and your various reactions as you are nervous, uncertain and trying to please us provides us with fuel. Once you begin to second guess it is a slippery slope which will lead to you becoming trapped in its nightmarish grip as you lose your sense of independence and identity. Should you find yourself in the position of second guessing you should recognise this for what it is; a further method of abusing you during devaluation.

45. Accuse You of Not Loving Us

As an empathic individual you are a love devotee. You believe in the concept of love and all the wonderful things that go with this emotion. It is also the case because of the way that we manipulate you, that you fall in love with us in a way you have not done so before. You fall deeply and completely in love with us. You do your very best to love us, showing us how much you care about us and you give us everything you can in order to make you and I come together as one. We know full well the effect the creation of our illusion has on you and we know that this affects you considerably. You are chosen at the outset as someone who is a love devotee and we know that you will pour your very being into loving us.

Accordingly, when we devalue you, we strike at one of the things which is very important to you. The concept of love. We aim to smash your belief in love as this will cause you to react in a heightened emotional manner. This means the fuel will flow from you as you cry, beg and increase the loving manner for which you are famed. The fuel you give off when we accuse you of not loving us is incredible Of course when we are accusing you of this a huge black flag is being waved under your nose. You do not notice it though because you are too preoccupied with proving to us that you do love us. If you stopped and actually stood back from what is happening and analysed it, you would see that our comments cannot stand up. You know you love us. You know you have done nothing to ever suggest that you have done anything but love us. You know that everything you do shows that you love us, yet as soon as we tell you that you do not love us any longer you fail to recognise the irrefutable logic of your position. Instead, as is so common with many of our manipulations, you will instead look to defend yourself and then prove yourself. You will react and give us fuel and thereafter you will double your efforts to show us that you love us. You are made to prove it, even though you already have done so. You go the extra mile, you put more effort in to trying to please us, make us happy and make us feel loved. It is in an impossible task but it is never enough. Once we have commenced your devaluation you cannot love us in the manner we want because all we want from you is the negative fuel. True, there will be occasions where we will take some positive fuel form you during a respite period, but it mainly becomes about the negative fuel. You do not see this and you flay yourself trying to convince us that you do love us. You are an honest person and you want to be believed. You hate not being believed. It offends you and this falls straight into our trap. A few choice comments, uttered in our usual confident and completely convinced manner is all that it takes for this particular abusive technique to be deployed and you are then a slave to trying to prove that we are wrong. Of course as you have learned by now, that we do not take kindly to being proved wrong and therefore you find yourself in an impossible position.

If your intimate partner levels this accusation at you, stop and consider whether it is really accurate. Chances are it is not and what you are dealing with is one of our abusive techniques wielded by our kind.

46 Won't Let You Sleep

This a particularly unpleasant yet effective method of doling out some abuse during the period of devaluation. Are you reading this through bleary eyes as you desperately await the effect of a caffeine boost to kick start your weary self into life to endure another day? Perhaps you can vividly recall that drained sensation that haunted you and that nagging ache which was ever present behind your eyeballs? The need to close your eyes and slip into a deep and restful slumber. All you wanted to do was to close your eyes and allow the tiredness to evaporate and shrouded in the amnesiac qualities of sleep you would be given respite from the nightmare that enveloped you. Yet, you were never able to achieve that sleep. Your near permanent anxiety meant that as you lay in bed you were tensed, ready to respond to the next jibe or manipulation. You heard a click. Was that me exiting the study at long last and coming to the bedroom or was it just the house settling? You were hyper vigilant and you cannot now recall how long that state had existed but you did know that if caused a nightly battle where you tried to sleep but each sound made you twitch and ready yourself. Sometimes you must have fallen asleep, such was the extent of your exhaustion and you dreamed and then suddenly you awoke. What had happened? Why did you awake so suddenly? You twist and see me there lying fast asleep, unburdened by any concerns. Even now you want to reach out and touch me in the hope that my hand will be placed on your shoulder and then my arm will envelope you, making you feel safe and secure, like it once did. You have learned not to reach out though for the consequences of waking me from my rest are not worth experiencing again. Instead, your shaking hand retreated and you turned to look at the clock and you sighed with resignation as you realised that the fitful sleep you had endured was only about an hour in length.

You lay there, eyes stinging and head heavy giving thanks that it was not one of those nights where I repeatedly jabbed you in the back to stop you sleeping. How did I manage to do that and then bound from the bed refreshed and revitalised as you rose like a zombie? How had I been able to interrupt your sleep through the night by prodding you and yet I was energetic? Was I sleeping during the day like some vampire hiding from the sunlight? At least this time I am sleeping and you have been spared the intermittent prod in the small of your back. It is a small mercy since the questions and thoughts race around your mind, as they always do in the dead of night. Why is this happening? What has gone wrong? Why am I doing this? When will it end? How can you stop it? Should you ask me to talk about it or will that risk another argument? How much more can you take? When did you last sleep properly? These questions and more besides whirl around in your mind, having taken a hold in your head. Your eyes flick to the silent television set in the corner of the room and you debate watching something, anything, just to break the relentless churning in your skull, but even with the volume set at barely audible you know it will disturb me and then it will be your fault again.

You look to the door now closed. You managed to resist a lock being fitted to the bedroom door, wary of what further horrors might be unleashed against you if your exit was barred but each day you fear that on your return that you will see an invoice from a joiner on the kitchen table and a lock has been fitted. You ponder whether you should head downstairs and see if sleep will come on the sofa or at least you can put the headphones on and listen to a radio play or some music. That would provide some sanctuary but yet again, as if possessed of some sixth sense, you know that I will appear and demand to know what you are doing downstairs in the middle of the night. No matter how deeply I appear to be sleeping it as if I sense your absence and come looking for you. It is then that you face the accusations of texting some man behind my back even though your 'phone is not to hand. It does not matter what the facts are does it? I always find a way of twisting the blame on to you. No, you cannot steal downstairs and instead you must remain board stiff in bed as your eyes watch the incessant march of time and sleep remains evasive. You can feel the hammering of your heart in your chest. Even though nothing is happening and all is quiet and still, that sense of foreboding remains. A cold hand of dread has gripped your heart and squeezes, driving the breath from your body and causing anxiety to spread across you. Perhaps you ought to see the doctor and see if he will prescribe something for this? You will need to do it without my knowledge otherwise I shall accuse you of attention-seeking by going to the doctor without consulting me first. I, of course, know what is best for you and I screen everything you do before determining whether I shall allow it. You know you ought to fight against it but you are so tired, so weary and you need what little strength remains to help you navigate a way throughout the day without treading on a mine and causing an explosion of fury. It is getting harder. You forget things now. Your memory used to be excellent or at least you think it did. Even thinking is becoming arduous and sometimes you just sit, staring into space, caught somewhere between wakefulness and hypnosis. If only one night of rest could come, if only this anxiety, this fear, this wariness would leave you and let you gain some strength, then you would not make the mistakes and I would not be angry. Perhaps then we could be as we used to be. You can still remember that and hope with all your heart that somehow this situation can be retrieved. You never felt tired then. You never walked with a shuffle or placed the milk in the dishwasher in error. You did not forget you were baking something until the acrid smell of smoke jolted you from your daydreaming and had you running into the kitchen, cursing your foolishness and immediately wondering if you could cook a fresh batch before I came home and witnessed another of your failures.

The clock shows 5am and sleep has evaded you once more. The dull throb in the centre of your forehead remains. You would have to be up in an hour anyway. There is no point trying to sleep now. You can see the first rind of dawn trying to permeate through the curtains and another day has arrived. You may as well rise and weave through this day, whichever day it is, is it Wednesday or Thursday? You cannot quite remember. You slide your feet from the bed and sit up, glancing at me over your shoulder, back now turned to you, my body rising and falling in a steady rhythm as I sleep on, oblivious to your exhaustion. You stand and sway a little as you ready yourself for another day of feeling drunk with fatigue.

The prevention of you gaining a good night's sleep is a clear method of abuse and another black flag which you should look out for as indicating that you are entangled with somebody who belongs to our club.

47 Iron Grip on Finances

This method of abuse focuses on the usual achievement of causing a reaction from you so that you provide fuel and allows us to exert control over you. It enables us to reinforce our superiority, it has you seeking approval from us to incur expenditure and by limiting your access to money it enables us to control your social life with the attendant benefits to us that I have described above. In respect of maintaining an iron grip on finances you need to aware of the following: -

-Insisting that all money goes into an account which we control

- Only allowing you a small amount of "spending money"

- Ensuring that you ask us for approval before incurring expenditure

-Limiting your access to credit cards

- Ensuring all assets are in our name

- Preventing you from working and thus denying you any form of potential financial independence

- Forcing you to "make do and mend" whilst we buy the newest and best for ourselves

- Annoyance if you incur expenditure without our prior approval

- Annoyance if you spend unnecessarily

- Insistence on reusing and re-cycling

We will always find ways of making our stance appear legitimate and if you dare to challenge us or question our stance concerning financial matters you can be assure that you will be met with ignited fury.

48 Comparisons with Others

This is another manifestation of triangulation. It is different from repeatedly mentioning somebody else which I referred to above. This is the frequent comparison, which will always be unfavourable of you to other people. You should watch out for the following indicators: -

- Praise for people on television and in films with associated comments that "you should be more like x or y"
- Praise for mutual acquaintances and again commenting that you should be more like this person, "Sandra has great fashion sense, it is such a shame that you cannot be like her."
- Praise for people we know you do not like and again comparing you to them.
- Praise for your friends and comparing you to them. This is a useful device for driving a wedge between you and them.
- Praise for family members (which will be done even if you know we do not like them) in order to compare their favourable attributes to your unfavourable ones
- Comparing things, you do, for example, if you follow a recipe in a cook book we will compare what you have cooked with the professional picture in the book in order to comment in a disparaging manner about your effort.
- Comparison between your achievements and ours which will always result in ours being superior to yours

These comparisons are carried out for the following reasons: -

- To cause you to react and provide us with fuel;
- To make you try harder so that there is a benefit to us (you look better, cook better, work harder, earn more money)

- To exert control over you;
- To erode your self-confidence and self-esteem and thus make you more susceptible to our other forms of manipulation.
- To reinforce our sense of superiority over you
- To reinforce your inferiority to you
- To punish you for being so poor in comparison to other people because we believe there is a risk that you will make us look poor in comparison owing to association
- To demonstrate that we think you are worthless

Where you find yourself being compared to others and this is done repeatedly and in an unfavourable fashion you should be aware that you are being subjected to a further form of abusive behaviour at the hands of a narcissist.

49 Turn People Against You

I have a busy day today. Much to do and many people to do it to but when you have someone's interests at heart, well, this is what you have to do isn't it? I have the list of telephone numbers which I have noted down from your telephone when I gained access to it. It was not difficult to do so. Using my famous ability to move around without making much of a noise I stole up behind you and watched you enter the passcode for your phone and I stored that in my memory to enable me to use it when you were sleeping. Naturally I had a good look through all your messages, your diary and e-mails but that is for another discussion. I recognised the names of numerous people and made a note of their numbers inside my little book and then hid that in readiness for when I decided it was time I needed to use it. Now that time has come and it is incumbent on me to take this step.

The first number I enter into my phone is that of Sarah, a friend of yours. She answers after two rings. Like many people she is surgically attached to the 'phone.

"Hello Sarah it is HG. Listen, I just wanted to let you know, since you are such a good friend of hers, that Gemma is, well I think the easiest way to describe it is that she is not well, not well at all. What do I mean? She has been acting rather strangely. The slightest thing seems to either have her shouting or crying. At first I wondered if it was just, you know, women's things, but it has been going on for months now. You had no idea? No I know, I have not said anything before because well I was hoping I could help her deal with it but it is beyond even me. I am going to get her some help. I try and talk to her about it but she just clams up on me, gives me silence and then a little later accuses me of not caring. I don't think she is sleeping properly either and it takes me an age to get her to eat. Should you come round? No, thank you, that is kind of you, but I don't want her to do anything which might upset you. She is very erratic in her behaviour but it is something more than just mood swings. I am going to get her the proper help but I am just forewarning you that if she contacts you just be aware that she is not herself. She has been saying things about people, me included, which are not very nice and I don't want this period of illness to affect her relationship with her friends, you know how some people can be overly sensitive to what someone says and they miss the point they are unwell. Yes, that's right. Yes, I think it would be a good idea if you just give her some space. Yes, absolutely. If she does contact me, let me know, you have my number on your 'phone now. Yes, I will pass on your kind words and thanks for your help Sarah, it is much appreciated at this difficult time."

I end the call and place a tick next to Sarah's name. She was most understanding and fully appreciate the need for space in order to allow you to get better. Now, who is next. Ah yes, another of your friends, Helen. I call Helen and explain the situation almost word-for-word as I did with Sarah. She asks more details about what is wrong and I reluctantly tell her about the violence and the lying. She is shocked I can tell and she spends some time searching for an amateur diagnosis as to what it might be. I listen as she drones on, checking my watch and noting I have other names to get through too. Eventually I am able to conclude the call and place another tick. I continue working my way through your list of friends, the ticks adding up. Next is John, your fitness instructor.

"Hello John, this is HG, Gemma's partner. We haven't met. Look John, difficult call to make but Gemma is unwell at present. It is pretty serious. Yes, thank you, it is a difficult time but I am doing the best I can to help her. It is unclear at present what it is, I am organising for a doctor to come and see her today but it is making her very difficult to be around. She may be suffering from some kind of breakdown brought on by exhaustion. Yes, it is a worry. I know you would not have thought it to look at her outside of our house but I think this has been brewing for some time, you know, she even started telling me that she was going to marry you. Yes, I know that is ridiculous isn't it? You are already married? I thought you were. Don't worry, I know nothing is going on, I am sure you are far too professional for that kind of thing, but this is part of the problem, she keeps coming out with outlandish comments and I can handle it but I worry others might not so she won't need your services until further notice. Payment? Well yes if she has an agreement with you then just continue to take her monthly payment after all this is not your fault is it? I will let you know when she is well again but just in case she tries to contact you I think it would be best if you don't take her calls, I don't want her causing you any trouble especially between you and your wife. Thank you John, your discretion is appreciated."

Another tick and a similar call is made to your choral group and your book club. Next is your employer. I made you take today off under the pretence of you gaining a lie in and then us doing something together. We stayed up late last night so you are still fast asleep upstairs allowing me to make these important telephone calls. Your employer is understanding and I can confirm that arrangements will be made to provide the relevant doctor's note because I explained this situation is likely to last a number of weeks. My preparation thus segues into arranging for the local doctor to make a house call after I explain to the receptionist, in worried tones, that having you leave the house in your current state might be a risk to both you and other people. She was most understanding and confirmed that a doctor would attend after surgery, around 5pm. Next on the list are your family members. I secured the advantage of persuading you to move with me away from them and they are now a flight away. The inconvenience of having to fly and the distance is something I play on as I call your parents and your sister, forewarning them that they may experience some unpleasant comments about them and especially me given her condition. I assure them that I am taking care of you and there is really no need for them to come all this way. I confirm I will keep them updated and they are pleased I have taken time off work to care for you and that I have arranged for a doctor to attend. I spend considerable time reeling off examples of the terrible behaviour you have exhibited, explaining the awful things I have been subjected to and the lies you have told about me, your friends and family. I explain that I can deal with it but I just feel so sorry for your parents and your sister having to hear such things and in order to prevent it happening again the best thing is to contact me and not you and to keep you at arms' length. I explain I understand that it is hard but it will be the best outcome for all concerned if you are prevented from lashing out and hurting people. My explanations and good intentions are accepted and thanks is offered for my understanding and support.

The final tick is placed on the list and I place both 'phone and pen down. I really should go and wash my hands now after smearing all that mud around.

This is a form of the smear campaign and should you become aware that we are doing this you should note that this is abusive but it also means that you are close to being discarded as we are reinforcing our façade and preparing to make you look like the crazy one in front of other people. We are priming these people to ensure that they do not believe you and prefer my version of events. We have decided that you are no longer functioning in the way that we require and we are going to cast you to one side, however before we do this, we want to turn people away from you or even against you.

50 Removing Things

If you find that things keep going missing and then re-appearing or they never appear at all, this is another form of abuse and is a manifestation of the technique of gas lighting, which I explained above. We do not recognise your possessions as belonging to you because we do not consider you as separate entity in your own right. We believe we are free to do what we want with items that belong to you. We may use them for ourselves or we may decide to purposefully hide items. This will cause upset and the provision of fuel if you think, for example, that an item that has sentimental value has been lost. It may never be found because we decided to sell it or even just throw it away. We may move objects around in order to create the impression that you are losing your mind (see above). We may purposefully remove our possessions in order to generate a pretext for accusing you of having moved them as we project our behaviour on to you and do so in order to create a scene. We may remove items in order to pretend they have been lost or stolen in order to make an insurance claim (against your policy).

We want to distress you, confuse you and annoy you. Removing items that belong to you, putting them somewhere else or never returning them is a way of exerting control over you and extracting fuel. It may be minor such as removing the television remote control so you are hunting all around for it before you try to settle down for an evening's viewing. It may be more significant as we move an important document, your purse or your car keys. Any way which enables us to create confusion in your mind as part of the gas lighting, makes you react so you provide us with fuel and demonstrates that we are the one pulling the strings (and thus in our minds it emphasises our superiority to you). We regard this as a perverted method of playing hide and seek as we remove items and laugh into our sleeves as we watching you hunting fruitlessly for the relevant item.

It you are subjected to this kind of behaviour, you are being manipulated by one of our kind and subjected to yet another form of unpleasant abuse.

Further required reading from H G Tudor

Evil

No Contact: How to Beat the Narcissist

Revenge: How to Beat the Narcissist

Adored and Abhorred

Sitting Target: How and Why the Narcissist Chooses You

Black Hole: The Narcissistic Hoover

A Grimoire of Narcissism

Cherished and Chastised

Red Flag: 50 Warning Signs of Narcissistic Seduction

Ask the Narcissist: The Answers to Your Questions

Darlings and Demons

All available on Amazon

Further interaction with H G Tudor

Knowing the Narcissist

@narcissist_me

Facebook

Narcsite.wordpress.com

Printed in Great Britain
by Amazon

74743243R00108